Explore The Rich History Of Pompeii City

Brooklyn H. Murphy

Introduction

This book takes you on an immersive journey through the captivating history of one of the most famous archaeological sites in the world. As you turn the pages of this book, you will uncover the mysteries and marvels of Pompeii, a city frozen in time by the eruption of Mount Vesuvius.

Our exploration begins with the earliest mentions of Pompeii in history, tracing its founding and early history. We delve into the conflicts that shaped the destiny of Pompeii, including the First Samnite War and the arrival of the Romans on its doorstep. Discover how the city's cultural heritage was influenced by various ancient civilizations, from the Oscans and Samnites to the Etruscans and Greeks.

Speaking of the Greeks, we unravel the profound impact of Greek culture on Pompeii, which left an indelible mark on its art, architecture, and way of life. You'll also encounter remnants of Egyptian culture within Pompeii's walls, showcasing the city's diverse cultural tapestry.

Step into the daily life of Pompeii's inhabitants under Roman rule. Explore the intricacies of their routines, from work and leisure to family life and religious practices. Meet some of the famous individuals who once called Pompeii home and learn about their contributions to the city's history.

But the heart of our narrative lies in the dramatic events leading up to the eruption of Mount Vesuvius. Walk the streets of Pompeii during its final days, and experience the mounting tension and anxiety that gripped its residents as the ominous volcano loomed over them.

The eruption of Mount Vesuvius is a climactic moment in Pompeii's history, and we guide you through the terrifying and destructive eruption that buried the city beneath layers of ash and pumice. Witness the tragic aftermath and the enduring legacy of this catastrophe.

This book is more than just a historical account; it is an opportunity to immerse yourself in the world of Pompeii, to feel the pulse of its ancient streets, and to witness the resilience of a city and its people, forever etched in history by the catastrophic forces of nature.

Contents

Chapter 1 – The First Mentions of Pompeii in History: The Founding of Pompeii

The city of Pompeii, along with the neighboring cities of Herculaneum and Stabiae, all found life and death in Mount Vesuvius. The soil in the surrounding area was fertile due to the presence of volcanic ash, so the Osci, also known as the Oscans, created an agricultural society in the Sarno Valley sometime between the 6th century and the 7th century BCE, although there is archaeological evidence of earlier settlements dating from the Iron Age, between the 8th century and the 9th century BCE. However, the earliest written evidence of the existence of Pompeii dates from the 6th century.

Pompeii was one of the rare settlements in this area that were not founded and inhabited by Greek colonists but were strongly influenced by Hellenic (Greek) culture. Aside from forming the village of Pompeii in the Sarno Valley to take advantage of the fertile soil, the Osci chose this area due to the naturally formed volcanic terraces that acted as a defense against potential intrusions and attacks from neighboring cities and villages. Not far from Pompeii, the Osci could extract water from the River Sarno, which contributed to the agricultural and societal development of the Osci and their settlements. Historians cannot say with certainty where the Oscans came from, but they do know the Osci belong to the Italic people and were an ethnic Indo-European group that spoke one of the Italic languages, specifically, the Oscan language.

The natural terraces formed by volcanic activity before the settlement of the Osci could not isolate the Oscans from Greek influence. Since Pompeii was surrounded by Greek colonies, it soon assimilated with the culture of ancient Greece, and it also gave in to Etruscan influence. The Doric Temple, which was erected in the Triangular Forum in Pompeii, stands as a physical witness to this cultural assimilation. It is also known that the Oscans and the Greek colony of Cumae in Campania established a commercial exchange. At the time, Pompeii received the status of an important trade center, which was how the Osci settlement became subject to Etruscan intrusions and expansion politics. The Etruscans penetrated the region of Campania and, with it, Pompeii. Pompeii was managed by the Osci at the time and had already been heavily influenced by the Hellenic culture through trade and the Greek colonization of the surrounding area. The Etruscans arrived around 650 BCE, coming from the north of Rome, and they became the leading force in the area, one that would last for more than fifty years. In the meantime, as the Etruscans spread their influence in Campania, the Greeks also extended their outreach in Campania, using Pompeii as a trading outpost rather than a colony since Pompeii was still a primitive settlement. Greek influence and colonies continued to expand across the Sarno Valley, affecting the native peoples in the area.

At the time, Greek colonies occupied the coastline and Campania as a whole, and as the Hellenic influence grew stronger with the power of the Greek colonies, the Greeks decided to drive the Etruscans out of Campania and Pompeii. In 474 BCE, the Etruscans suffered a defeat in the Battle of Cumae against the Greek colonies of Syracuse and Cumae. Cumae was the first Greek settlement in the mainland of Italy, and it was formed and colonized around the 8th century BCE. By 474 BCE, Cumae had become one of the strongest if not the strongest Greek colony in Italy.

Back in 504 BCE, before the Battle of Cumae, the Etruscans had tried to war against Cumae but failed. Even though they were weakened, the Etruscans managed to recollect their naval forces to launch a direct attack on Cumae, as they wanted to expand their territories to southern Italy.

The people of Cumae called for military assistance from Hieron I of Syracuse to drive the Etruscans out of the Bay of Naples. During the reign of Hieron I, who is known as the tyrant of Syracuse, the power of Syracuse was increased greatly, which was why Syracuse was a worthy opponent to the Etruscans.

After the great defeat of the Etruscan forces, Hieron ended the battle as a hero, later dedicating a bronze helmet from the battlefield at Olympus to commemorate the event that saved the Greek colonies from the Etruscans' expanding influence. After the battle, the Etruscans not only lost their political influence but also their positions on the sea. Their territories were soon taken by the arriving Samnites, Romans, and Gauls.

In 440 BCE, the territories that had once belonged to the Etruscans were slowly occupied by the Samnites. The Samnites were an Italic people. They were related to the Osci and even spoke a similar language, although they never identified with the Oscans. The Samnites arrived from the harsh Apennine Mountains located in central Italy and occupied Pompeii. Both Pompeii and Herculaneum became a part of the Samnite territories in the 5th century BCE as the power shifted from the Etruscans to the Greeks to finally the Samnites before the Roman occupation took place.

The Samnites had a plan to commercialize the area and use it for trading, and they established dominance over the Mediterranean to control the lowlands and the Tyrrhenian Sea. After taking Pompeii, the Samnites built a thriving city with homes, ritual buildings, and a two-mile city wall to protect Pompeii from potential attacks and intrusions. The Samnites also buried their dead within the strongholds of Pompeii. The oldest grave excavated in Pompeii so far belonged to a thirty-five-year-old to a forty-year-old Samnite woman of unknown origins and social class. Pompeii slowly became the jewel in the Samnites' crown of Campania and the surrounding area, as the city thrived during the rule of this Italic civilization.

Nearly a hundred years after the Samnites occupied Pompeii and Campania, the Romans arrived. In 343 BCE, armed conflicts commenced between the Samnites, Romans, and Greeks. The great melting pot that was created by these multiple power shifts eventually reached its boiling point.

The First Samnite War and the Arrival of the Romans at Pompeii

The Roman Republic (510–27 BCE) was already taking an interest in the area of Campania as a part of the republic's expansionist and diplomatic politics. When the Romans arrived at Pompeii, the Samnites represented the dominant force in the region, as they were still expanding across Campania and attacking the surrounding cities. One such city was Capua, which was located in southern Italy and was a part of the Campania region. The Romans' arrival to Campania was most likely the result of the Campanians and the cities that were suffering attacks from the Samnites pleading for outside assistance. At the time, the Roman Republic had not expressed much of an interest in expanding to the region of Campania.

In 343 BCE, the series of battles known to history as the Samnite Wars commenced. The first armed encounter between the Romans and the Samnites is known as the Battle of Mount Gaurus (Mount Gaurus is also known as Mount Barbaro). Titus Livius, better known as simply Livy, the famous Roman historian, described the battle in the *History of Rome*, which was written in Latin between 27 BCE and 9 BCE. Modern historians argue that many events regarding the Battle of Mount Gaurus were mostly invented either by Livy's sources or the historian himself.

At the time of the First Samnite War, the Roman Republic was led by two elected Roman consuls: Marcus Valerius Corvus and Aulus Cornelius Cossus.

Marcus Valerius Corvus was elected as a consul six times. He was first elected at the age of twenty-three, and he was only twenty-seven when he led his army, which joined with Aulus Cornelius Cossus's army, against the Samnites. Corvus was also appointed as dictator two times and was an important military commander and politician in the Roman Republic. Corvus was a member of the gens Valeria. The gens Valeria was a prominent patrician (ruling class) family of ancient Rome, and they were influential from the beginning of the Roman Republic to the end of the Roman Empire.

The other consul, Aulus Cornelius Cossus, who also led his army into the Battle of Mount Gaurus, was a member of the gens Cornelia. The gens Cornelia was one of the oldest patrician families in ancient Rome, and it was famous for producing at least seventy-five consuls. For seven hundred years, the house from which Aulus Cornelius Cossus originated produced more generals and statesmen than any other patrician family in all of Rome.

What the Samnites could not predict upon attacking the northern tribe of Campania known as the Sidicini was that the Romans would meddle with their plans of invasion and break the treaty. At the time, the Roman Republic had a treaty with the Samnites, although the exact terms weren't listed by any of the relevant historians of the era. A condition that was known, however, was that the Liris River represented a border that shouldn't be crossed by either the Romans on its north banks or the Samnites in the south. However, the republic ignored the treaty once they were summoned to aid the Campanians. Before pleading for the Romans to come help against the invading Samnites, the city-state of Capua tried to defend the Sidicini but was beaten in battle. The republic then declared war against the Samnites, and Valerius arrived at Mount Gaurus, where he set up his military camp.

The Samnites moved to Campania with all their might and force, and Valerius utilized his position to test the enemy's strength with light infantry and light cavalry, known as skirmishers. Neither side could gain the upper hand, so Valerius decided to send the Roman cavalry in full charge to try and break the Samnite lines.

The cavalry had to retreat when the Samnites attacked with a greater force. With this failed counterattack behind him, Valerius decided to lead the infantry in person in another attempt to break the

Samnite forces. Livy states this second attempt also failed, but Valerius did not give up, charging forward with another attack. The Samnites chose to retreat, and the Romans fully took their camp by the next morning.

Even though the Romans won the battle against the Samnites, the war was yet to be won. The second battle of the First Samnite War was the Battle of Saticula. This time around, the Roman military forces were led by Consul Aulus Cornelius Cossus. Saticula was one of the Samnite cities at the time, and it was located near the frontier of Campania. As described by Livy, Cossus and his men were attacked by Samnite forces in a mountain pass after marching from the city of Saticula. Livy writes that one of the Roman military tribunes, Publius Decius Mus, led a group of men to the top of the hill to distract the enemy forces so that the consul could flee with the army.

However, as with the other Samnite battles, modern historians doubt the events Livy describes in the *History of Rome*; unfortunately, Livy's book is the only source that details the battles in any depth. Another reason historians doubt Livy's version of the Battle of Saticula is the fact that there is a strong similarity to the resolution of another battle in the First Punic War, where the Roman army was also saved by a distraction made by a military tribune.

The third and last battle of the First Samnite War was led by Corvus and is known as the Battle of Suessula. Suessula was an ancient city located in southern Campania, and it was also the place where the Samnites gathered their military forces ahead of the last battle. Corvus responded to the gathering by marching his forces to Suessula to seize the opportunity and attack the enemy. Livy is once again the only source that describes the battle and claims that the Roman army launched an attack on the Samnite camp once a part of their army went foraging for food. Both Corvus and Cossus were rewarded with a triumph (a victory parade) once they got back to Rome, the "Eternal City."

In 341 BCE, the Roman Senate responded to the Samnites' appeal to reflect on the former treaty it had with Rome and agreed to peace.

The Second and Third Samnite Wars

The Second Samnite War commenced in 326 BCE after the Roman Republic declared war against the Samnites after the Samnites were unable to prevent their subjects from attacking and raiding the city of Fregellae, a city located in Latium where the Roman Republic had a colony. The war lasted until 304 BCE, ending with a victory for Rome.

In 310 BCE, the city of Pompeii is first mentioned in Roman records. During the Second Samnite War, the Roman fleet arrived to one of the ports in Pompeii, known as Sarno. The fleet had intentions to launch an attack on the neighboring city of Nuceria, which turned out to be futile for the Romans. The Roman fleet pillaged the city of Nuceria, but they found it difficult to subdue it, despite its great strategic position from the port of Pompeii.

In 300 BCE, each city of Campania arranged an individual treaty with Rome, forming a confederation and granting the cities the status of allies with complete rights to have an independent government. The Samnite culture, however, was still dominant in the area, which included Pompeii.

Only a year later, in 299 BCE, the Etruscans prepared to wage war against Rome. It is presumed that the reason behind this was the fact that Rome had set up a colony near Umbria in Narnia (Narni). These plans were intercepted by the Gauls when they invaded Etruscan territory. The Etruscans offered them an alliance in which they would pay for their support, and the Gauls agreed. The Etruscans counted on their alliance with the Gauls to help them win the war against Rome. However, the Gauls disagreed with fighting a war against Rome, stating that the agreement only referred to not claiming or devastating Etruscan territory. As a result, the Etruscans dismissed the Gauls, paying and releasing them from their agreement.

At the same time, the Samnites were also preparing for war, of which the Romans were warned by their new allies, the Picentes, the people who lived in today's territory of modern-day Marche on the Adriatic coast.

Rome sent an army to Etruria in 299 BCE, with consul Titus Manlius Torquatus at its head. He was fatally injured in a riding accident on his way to Etruria. The Etruscans believed that this event was an omen when it came to waging war against Rome. Rome soon sent a replacement for the deceased consul: Marcus Valerius Corvus, who was the consul during the First Samnite War. Despite the Etruscans' beliefs, the Roman army ravaged Etruria; however, the Etruscans refused to leave their fortifications.

In the meantime, in 298 BCE, a Lucanian delegation traveled to Rome to ask the Romans to protect them against the Samnites, who had invaded their territory and threatened their safety. The Romans agreed and formed yet another alliance. Lucania was the land of the Lucanians, who were an Oscan-speaking people living in the area from the Tyrrhenian Sea to the Gulf of Taranto. An order was sent to the Samnites to leave the Lucanian territory at once. However, the Samnites refused and once again threatened the safety of the Lucanians. Due to the treaty it had made with the Lucanians, Rome intervened, openly declaring war on the Samnites. Some historians suggest that it was in the best interests of Rome to start another war with Samnium (the region of southern Italy inhabited by the Samnites), which was why they deliberately formed alliances with the Samnites' enemies. At the same time, Rome probably feared that the Samnites would only grow stronger if they managed to subdue the Lucanians.

The Romans defeated the Etruscans in a battle near Volterra in 298 BCE. The only source of the battle is once again Livy; however, it seems there are few inconsistencies, even though there are no parallel sources to which to compare Livy's records.

The elections for the next pair of consuls took place in 297 BCE, around the time rumors were spreading that the Samnites and Etruscans were gathering huge armies against Rome and were planning to come as far as the Eternal City. Wanting to prepare for the rumored conflict, the Romans sought to elect Quintus Fabius Maximus Rullianus.

Rullianus was certainly the most experienced military commander in Rome; however, he refused to become a consul unless Publius Decius Mus became his colleague consul. The two had also been elected as consuls together in 308 BCE. Rome obliged, and the pair were sent off to war.

In the meantime, the news of Etruria suing for peace arrived in Rome, which meant that Rullianus and Decius Mus could march their armies to Samnium. In 297 BCE, the Battle of Tifernum took place in the valley near Tifernum. The Samnites were prepared to launch an attack against Rome, but Publius Decius Mus intercepted their plans by setting up his military camp at Maleventum, a city in Campania where an Apulian army was supposed to join the Samnites in their attack against Rome. Rome ended the battle in victory.

In 296 BCE, Appius Claudius Caecus and Lucius Volumnius Flamma Violens were elected as consuls, although the previous consuls had their consulship extended for six more months. They served as proconsuls, which allowed them to carry out the war against the Samnites. Decius Mus went on to attack the Samnite territories, mostly ravaging the surrounding villages to intimidate the Samnites.

In the meantime, the Samnites asked the Etruscans for an alliance or, at the very least, aid. The Samnites emphasized that they were not able to defeat Rome by themselves and that by combining the riches of one of the wealthiest nations in Italy with the power of the Samnite armies, they could drive the Romans out of Campania.

The Etruscan cities voted in favor of war while the Samnites gathered a massive army. Publius Decius Mus was, by this point, attacking the Samnite cities; however, there were no recorded triumphs for the consuls of Rome at the time, prolonging the conflict for yet another year.

Before the decisive Battle of Sentinum took place, the Samnites raided the cities of Roman allies across Campania, which urged Rome to take further action. In the meantime, the Etruscans were gathering their forces, joining their armies with the Gauls, Umbrians, and Samnites. This was the first time that Rome faced an enemy alliance of four different nations.

To prepare against one of the biggest battles Rome had ever seen, Publius Decius Mus and Quintus Fabius Maximus Rullianus were elected as consuls once again for their exceptional military command. The command of Lucius Volumnius Flamma Violens was also extended for another year—Rome needed to win so it could remain influential in Campania. Rullianus and Decius Mus combined their armies with the allied forces from Campania, which would be led to Etruria. Violens was sent to Samnium with two legions.

Even though the Samnites created a powerful coalition with the Gauls, Umbrians, and Etruscans, Rome won the Battle of Sentinum, thus winning the Samnite Wars and allowing them to establish their dominance in central Italy. It appears that the coalition was not ready for Rome. Although the Romans lost eight thousand soldiers in the battle, the allied Samnite forces lost twenty thousand men. The consuls returned to Rome victorious and were celebrated in a triumph.

The Aftermath of the Roman-Samnite Conflicts

These battles and frequent shifts of power created a unique and versatile cultural history that impacted the city of Pompeii. However, before Roman power was firmly established in Pompeii, Rome would face more challenges. For although Rome won the Battle of Sentinum, the Samnites were not ready to give up on Campania just yet.

The Samnites raided three Roman armies in 294 BCE, one of which was supposed to return to Etruria, the second to defend the borders, and the third to raid Campania. The Samnites attacked the Romans in the fog, killing many men and several officers. The Romans managed to repel the Samnites, but they were unable to pursue them due to the fog.

In 293 BCE, Spurius Carvilius Maximus was elected as one of the consuls, and he took experienced troops to take over Amiternum, which was located in Samnium. The other elected consul was Lucius Papirius Cursor, whose father had led Roman troops in the Second Samnite War. Lucius Papirius Cursor led his troops in an attack on Duronia, taking the Samnite city by storm. These types of conflicts would remain until 290 BCE, when the last Samnite stands of resistance would be overtaken by the Roman armies.

Pompeii would remain heavily influenced by the Greeks and the Oscans until after the Social Wars in 89 BCE, when the Oscan language was replaced with Latin and heavily transformed by Roman culture. As a punishment for participating in the Social Wars, Pompeii was first turned into a Roman colony of war veterans, serving as a military garrison before becoming known as one of the wealthiest cities in Campania.

Chapter 2 – Cultural Heritage That Formed Pompeii and Survived the Influence of Rome

When talking about the history of Pompeii, there is a great emphasis on the culture and heritage of Rome since Pompeii was under Roman rule at the time of the famous eruption that "froze" the ancient world and its inhabitants in time until excavations commenced in 1738, over 1,500 years after the eruption of Vesuvius.

When observing the name of the city, "Pompeii," we can see how the Latin language shaped the form of the word (Pompeii, -orum). However, the origin of the word is found in the Oscan language, *pompe*, which means five in Oscan. It is believed the city consisted of five hamlets (smaller settlements or villages).

By studying language morphology and the origins of the city's name, historians can determine that the Oscan people once inhabited Pompeii and that the Oscan heritage remained in the very foundation of the city even after the arrival of the Romans. The Samnites were also one of the first people to inhabit Pompeii, and their cultural heritage also survived the tooth of time.

At the very beginning of the city's history, fertile lands and rain contributed to the development of early agricultural settlements. Still, archaeologists are finding new evidence of the first civilizations that lived in the city, and the image they previously had about the life and culture of the Samnites is changing with new discoveries. But let us start with the first civilization to influence Pompeii: the Oscans.

The Oscans (Osci)

It is believed the Oscans founded five smaller villages on the location of Pompeii in the 8th century BCE, and it is presumed that they were the first people to inhabit the city and utilize its natural riches. The city was built 40 meters (around 131 feet) above sea level on a coastal plateau created by earlier eruptions of Mount Vesuvius. The plateau declined into the sea to the west with a steep fall to the south. Pompeii once bordered the coastline but is now seven hundred meters away from the coast.

Sadly, the remains of the Oscan culture could not defy time and decay. The only remains of the Oscan heritage in Pompeii are found in literary references, place names, and a small number of Roman scriptures. Historians and archaeologists cannot know with certainty how the Oscans lived or what their buildings looked like. It is presumed that the first settlements were primitive, given the time the city of Pompeii was founded. However, the cultural legacy of the Osci remains in the name of Pompeii, as it is thought they built the five hamlets that once made the foundation of the city.

As a civilization, the Oscans were just not strong enough and lacked the military power and riches needed to repel invaders, namely the Romans. They managed to maintain their independence for many years, mostly by finding ways to play one state against another; for instance, the Oscans did this to the Samnites and Romans during the Samnite Wars.

After the Second Samnite War, the Oscans lost their independence against the Romans and quickly assimilated with their culture when Rome decided to secure the tribes that thrived on the border. What might have made the assimilation of the Oscans with Roman culture easier was the fact that the Oscan language was closely related to Latin. Still, the Oscan language evolved after the Romans arrived in Campania, and it was used by several sovereign tribal states, such as the Samnites, Sidicini, and Aurunci. The Sidicini and Aurunci were often referred to as the "Osci."

Oscan graffiti has been found on the walls of Pompeii, which indicates that the language was still spoken in the city into the 1st century BCE, beyond the Samnite Wars. One of the oldest pieces of evidence written in Oscan dates back to the 5th century BCE. This is the Tabula Bantina, which translated from Latin means "Tablet from Bantia." The Tabula Bantina is one of the major sources of the ancient Oscan language, with text on both sides of the bronze tablet. The inscription on one side is written in Latin, while the other side is written in Oscan. The tablet dates somewhere between 150 BCE and 100 BCE.

The Samnites

The Samnites also spoke the Oscan language; however, the Samnites never identified themselves as Oscans, nor were the Oscans known as Samnites. The Samnites lived in a region of southern Italy, which was known among the Romans as Samnium. The Samnites also formed a confederation with other tribes in the region: the Pentri, Caraceni, Caudini, and Hirpini.

The Samnites and Romans were not always enemies, as they formed an alliance against the Gauls in 354 BCE. However, the Samnites later became enemies of Rome, and the two forces clashed in a series of wars known as the Samnite Wars. After Rome ended the wars in victory, the Samnites helped the enemies of Rome, including a Greek king named Pyrrhus, who waged war against the Roman Republic between 280 BCE and 275 BCE. Some Samnites even joined forces with Hannibal Barca in the Second Punic War, which lasted from 218 BCE to 201 BCE.

The Samnites fought Rome once again with other Italic tribes in the Social Wars in 91 BCE. At the time, many of these cities and tribes were allies of Rome, and the reason for waging war against the Roman Republic was the fact that they wanted to have Roman citizenship. Rome did not want to grant Roman citizenship to the various Italic tribes, and as a punishment, the Republic declared war. The Social Wars ended in 87 BCE, and the Romans began their efforts to bring all of Italy under their thumb. (The Social Wars will be discussed in more depth in a later chapter.)

Before the Samnites were completely Latinized and had assimilated with Roman culture, Pontius Telesinus, a Samnite military leader, made one last attempt to lead his people into battle against Roman domination. He was one of the rebel military commanders who fought in the Social Wars, and he also intervened in the Roman civil wars in the hopes of gaining a better position. However, in his attempt to do so, he was killed in a battle against Sulla, a Roman general, in 82 BCE. After Telesinus died, the Samnites scattered. (As an interesting side note, some historians claim that Pontius Telesinus might have been an ancestor of Pontius Pilatus, the Roman governor of Judea who ordered the execution of Jesus Christ.)

After the Samnite defeat, Sulla ordered that anyone who played a role in the rebellion should be hunted, severely punished, and killed. Due to this order, many Samnite cities were turned into small villages, and some were destroyed and/or deserted. With this turn of events, the Samnites lost their political importance, and they completely submitted to the Romans.

On the cultural front, a team of European archaeologists discovered a pre-Roman temple in 2005 during an excavation, which revealed a new image of the Samnite people. The Samnites were mostly described in history, at least in the surviving sources, as mountain folk and warriors that thrived thanks to their pact with Rome before the start of the Samnite Wars. A strong militaristic nature was what characterized the Samnites in history until the 2005 discovery of a temple in Pompeii dedicated to the Samnite goddess Mephitis (Mefitis).

The temple was built sometime around the 3rd century BCE and was dedicated to the goddess of swamps, although she was also celebrated as the goddess of underground water sources and springs. The fact that many of these underground sources were sulfurous led the people to associate Mephitis with volcanic vapor and poisonous gases, so it is no wonder that Mephitis was worshiped in Pompeii, a city with a view of Mount Vesuvius. The Romans embraced the temple and adopted it after colonizing the city in 80 BCE. Temples dedicated to Mephitis were also found in Samnium, Cremona, and Esquiline Hill in Rome.

The Etruscans

The earliest evidence of Etruscans dates back to 900 BCE, the period of the Iron Age in central and northern Italy, known as the Villanovan culture. With the ending of the Villanovan phase, the Etruscans fell under the influence of the ancient Greeks around 750 BCE.

The Etruscans were known as Tyrrhenians to the Greeks, while the Romans referred to the Etruscans as Tusci, which, translated from Latin, means "people who build towers." This name fits the Etruscans well, as they often built their towns on cliffs and surrounded them with tall walls.

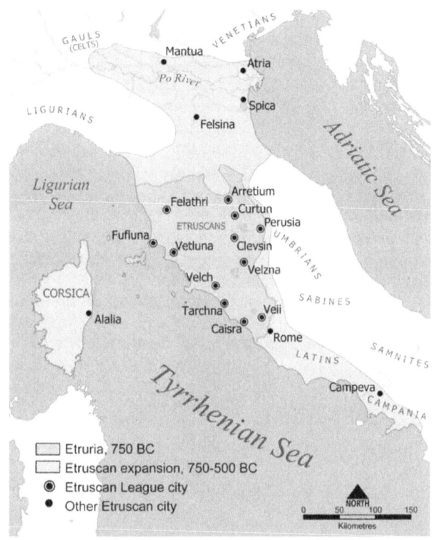

Etruscan civilization and the league of twelve Etruscan cities (900 BCE to 750 BCE).
NormanEinstein, CC BY-SA 3.0 <http://creativecommons.org/licenses/by-sa/3.0/>, via Wikimedia Commons
https://commons.wikimedia.org/wiki/File:Etruscan_civilization_map.png

Around 500 BCE, with the arrival of the Romans, any political balance of power that the Etruscans might have held shifted to the Roman Republic. Before the Romans arrived, every city in Etruria had an independent government, with noble families most likely posing as the city's rulers. The Etruscan families earned their riches through trading with the Celtic people and the Greeks, which gave them more than enough capital for their luxurious tombs, which were filled with all kinds of goods, valuables, and artwork.

The connection between the Romans and Etruscans goes back to the very founding of Rome and the first supposed king of Rome: Romulus. It is hard to sort fact from fiction when it comes to Romulus, but this book will assume that he ruled from 753 BCE to 716 BCE. According to legend, sometime in the 8th century BCE, during Romulus's reign, the Fidenates, an Etruscan people who lived in Fidenae, an ancient town of Latium located only eight kilometers (five miles) north of Rome, wanted to remove the menace that Rome was threatening to become. So, they decided to lay waste to the land. Romulus responded to that provocation by marching with his army to Latium. Romulus set up an ambush and waited for the Fidenates to leave the city. Once that happened, Romulus took the town by surprise.

Former Etruscan town of Bagnoregio, Latium, Italy. Jonathan Fors.

The Roman-Etruscan conflicts continued in the Roman-Etruscan Wars, which took place under both the Kingdom of Rome and the Roman Republic. The last resistance of the Etruscan people was crushed in 264 BCE, and Etruria was finally under the influence of Rome. However, the Etruscans managed to leave an imprint on the culture of Rome. To testify to the influence of the Etruscans, the common word "person," which exists in many cultures in the same or similar form, might be derived from an Etruscan word, *phersu*. *Phersu* means either "mask" or "masked man." Some scholars believe it could possibly mean "actor" since Etruscan actors wore masks.

More reminders of Etruscan civilization survived Roman colonization and assimilation, such as architecture, statues, sarcophagi, tombs, and art. The Etruscan concept of large villas with spacious gardens, as well as arched gates and large temples, was adopted by other cities and states in Italy. However, there is no substantial evidence of any Etruscan architectural remains in Pompeii, suggesting that many of the Etruscan buildings were completely removed and demolished to make space for those built by the Romans.

The center of the Etruscan society was the married couple, and monogamy was enforced. Thus, tombs were seldom made as individual resting places; couples were often buried together in the same sarcophagus, with the idea that monogamous pairings in the afterlife would be celebrated and cherished.

Unlike in Greece and Rome at the time, respectable women of Etruria could freely socialize with men, although this freedom might have been confused with vulgar availability in the eyes of Greeks and Romans, whose respectable women spent their time inside their homes. The fact that both the names of the mother and the father was written on Etruscan tombs emphasizes the importance of female figures, especially mothers, in Etruscan culture.

The Etruscan Sarcophagus of the Spouses; the Louvre, Paris, France.
Louvre Museum, CC BY-SA 3.0 <http://creativecommons.org/licenses/by-sa/3.0/>, via Wikimedia Commons https://commons.wikimedia.org/wiki/File:Paris_-_Louvre_-_Sarcophage.jpg

The Greeks

Hellenic influence in Pompeii and Campania started with Greek colonization, which took place between the 8th and 6th centuries BCE. According to the numerous findings over the years, the Greeks had established their culture in Pompeii by the 8th century BCE, at the very beginning of their colonization. At the time, Greeks were expanding to the Black Sea and the Mediterranean Sea, as well as southern Italy.

During the 8th century BCE, the Greeks occupied the coastal area of southern Italy, inhabiting not only Campania, where the city of Pompeii was located, but also the regions of Calabria, Basilicata, Apulia, and Sicily. Many native civilizations in these regions were Hellenized during the period of colonization and adopted Greek culture. The Greeks, for the most part, organized colonies in southern Italy due to the need for new ports and outposts that would improve trading, aid in finding new resources and raw materials, and make the colonization process smoother.

In part, colonization was necessary for the Greeks at the beginning, as many moved to Italy to escape famine and overcrowding. Greek colonization was also driven by the civil wars that affected many Greek city-states on the mainland. These civil wars were known as stasis. Staseis happened throughout all of Greece, with political opposition against the ruling party rising up to decry economic or social problems. When Greek colonization first started, tyrannical authorities were taking power in mainland Greece; as a result, many early Greek colonists were political exiles.

Due to colonization, the Greeks exported their culture to southern Italy. However, the Hellenic culture developed further from that point, interacting with the many Italic civilizations and their cultural characteristics.

In Rome, the regions that were inhabited by Greek colonists were known as Magna Graecia, which means "Greater Greece," as southern Italy was densely populated by the Greeks. Greek colonists created city-states that became very rich and powerful over time, some of which still stand to testify to the glory of the ancient Greeks who colonized the Italian Peninsula.

The Greek colonists adapted to their new environment and successfully influenced the Italic civilizations that were native to the region. In addition, the Greek colonies contributed to the development and growth of the metropolises by strategically directing colonists to new areas that should be colonized. Establishing new colonies was something that was carefully planned to provide secure and beneficial conditions for future and current colonists. The area of a future colony would be carefully analyzed, and if it passed the inspection, which looked at the area's usefulness and advantages, colonists would arrive to build in the region. One of the leading criteria for choosing future colonies was safety from raiders and attackers.

The Greeks did not establish a colony directly in Pompeii, although the city of Pompeii was near one of the biggest Greek colonies in Italy, Naples, also known as Neapolis ("New City") in the ancient world. As you can imagine, Hellenic influence must have been strong in Pompeii due to its proximity to Naples, which is about 25.5 kilometers (about sixteen miles) from Pompeii. At the same time, since the Greeks did not directly colonize the city of Pompeii, it was somewhat independent in the cultural and political sense.

Ancient Greece was one of the greatest early opponents of Rome. However, despite political conflicts and later wars and battles between Greek colonies and Rome, the Romans did not hide their fascination with Hellenic culture, and they did not seem to mind the influential culture and religion of the ancient Greeks. After the Roman Kingdom was overthrown, the Roman Republic started to take over Greek city-states and colonies, with Neapolis being the first to be taken by Rome in 327 BCE. Rome then conquered other Greek colonies, continuing their expansion during the Samnite Wars and the Pyrrhic War (the war waged by the aforementioned King Pyrrhus). The last colony to fall under Roman rule was Taras (today's Taranto) in 272 BCE. Syracuse was the only Greek colony to remain independent during the bulk of Roman expansion, thanks to the friendly political relations between Rome and the king of Syracuse, Hiero II (r. 270–215 BCE). Syracuse lost its independence in 212 BCE due to its king, Hieronymus (the grandson of Hiero II), granting an alliance to one of Rome's enemies, the famous Carthaginian general Hannibal.

It is amazing to think about how Pompeii was touched and

influenced by so many civilizations. When one civilization left, another swooped in to take its place, melding their culture with what had once been there. The excavations of Pompeii have revealed a rich cultural history, and we will now look at that history, with a larger emphasis being placed on the Greek culture, which was adopted and preserved by the Romans long after the Greek colonies were conquered.

Chapter 3 – The Greeks in Pompeii: Culture, Architecture, Art, Religion, Literature, and Drama

Pompeii was founded by the Oscan people and was later shaped and developed over the years by numerous cultures that were drawn to the region of Campania and southern Italy, mostly because of trading opportunities and agricultural riches. While traces of all these cultures can still be found in Pompeii under layers of volcanic sediment that buried the entire city in 79 CE, the Hellenic culture is still the most dominant in Pompeii, with numerous testimonies of Roman appreciation for Greek culture, which included their opulent architecture, art, religion, literature, and drama. The Romans valued the Greek culture so much that they made sure to adopt and preserve it.

The Legacy of Greek Culture in Pompeii

The influence of Greek culture can be seen in the architectural composition of Pompeii. While most of the preserved buildings were built by the Romans after their conquest of southern Italy, they were heavily influenced by the Hellenic and Hellenistic architectural styles. To make the difference between the two clear for readers, Hellenic refers to the people of ancient Greece before Alexander the Great's death in 323 BCE, while Hellenistic refers to the period after Alexander the Great's death and the rise of the Roman Empire. The Hellenistic style incorporates influences from the East, namely west and central Asia, with Greek culture.

The Basilica in Pompeii might be one of the most splendid buildings in the Forum that was uncovered during the excavations. In the time of the Roman Republic and later the Roman Empire, the Basilica was used for the administration of justice and city business. The Basilica also features an imposing decorated suggestum, which was a platform where the judges would be seated while managing judicial affairs. The Basilica was most likely built between 130 BCE and 120 BCE, and it shows clear Greek influence through the use of its Ionic and Corinthian columns, which was characteristic of Greek architecture. In the center of the Basilica's interior was a statue of a horse rider, complimented with surrounding walls decorated with stucco, which was often used for decorating walls in ancient Greece and Rome.

The influence of Greek culture on architecture in Pompeii is also seen in the Palestra (or Palaetra), which was built by the Romans in the eastern part of the city. Palestras, which means "gyms," were often used by the Romans for exercise and training; these structures originate from the Greeks, who called them *gymnasions* ("gymnasium" is the Latinized version of the word). The Palestra in Pompeii was probably built between 40 BCE and 20 CE, sometime during the Augustan Age.

The streets of Pompeii were also inspired by the Greeks. The Pompeiians used insulae to divide the city into blocks. Insulae is a city block that can also refer to a house similar to an apartment building. The streets were built in a way so that all the city districts were seamlessly connected through the use of insulae, and it allowed several main streets to be inventively interconnected with a great number of smaller streets.

The affinity the rich and powerful inhabitants of Pompeii had for Greek culture is witnessed in the use of peristyles, which were inspired by the Greeks. The peristyle is a columned walkway that surrounds either a courtyard or a part of a building, typically around an enclosed garden. Many villas and private homes that were unveiled hundreds of years after the eruption of Mount Vesuvius had peristyles surrounding gardens.

The House of the Faun, featuring two different kinds of peristyles built during different periods of time, Pompeii, Carol Raddato.
Carole Raddato from FRANKFURT, Germany, CC BY-SA 2.0

The House of the Faun

The House of the Faun, one of the most elaborate villas that have been uncovered in Pompeii, uses two peristyle systems; the

peristyles were built during different timeframes during the 2nd century BCE. The House of the Faun is a rather important piece of archaeological evidence, as it provides us with a glimpse of life in Pompeii during the time the Roman Republic established itself as a predominant force in the region. Historians and archaeologists claim that the House of the Faun stands as the perfect testament of life in the Roman Republic. Since the House of the Faun was buried in the residue of volcanic ash from the eruption that destroyed the city, artwork, such as the House of the Faun's famed mosaics, and other artifacts were left, for the most part, intact. German archaeologists began the initial excavations of the House of the Faun in 1830, and the treasures they unearthed were priceless to scholars.

The House of the Faun got its name after an archaeological excavation revealed a statue of a dancing faun made from bronze. It was found at the front of the impluvium, which is a part of the house intended for collecting rainwater. The fact that the Romans would choose a faun, the protector of forests and untamed life of the woodlands, also testifies to the influence of Greek culture, as the Romans often connected fauns to Greek satyrs (fauns are typically depicted as half-human, half-goat, while satyrs are usually depicted as men with horse-like features).

Archeologists also discovered insignia bearing the name of Saturninus, indicating that an important and old Roman *gens*, the Satria, lived in this lavish house. They also found a ring bearing the name of the gens Cassius. Cassius was a Roman family name during great antiquity. This evidence suggests that someone from gens Cassius married someone from the Satria family and that they made the House of the Faun their home.

A copy of the dancing faun statue found in the House of the Faun.
sabrina roberjot, CC BY-SA 3.0 <http://creativecommons.org/licenses/by-sa/3.0/>, via Wikimedia Commons
https://commons.wikimedia.org/wiki/File:StatueFaunePomp%C3%A9i.JPG

Although the House of the Faun is an exceptional piece of Greek-inspired Roman aristocratic housing, the house was originally built during the period the Samnites inhabited the city. The house was not used for a while after the Samnites left the area, but it was later renovated to house the family of Satria. The size of the house also speaks on behalf of aristocratic life in Pompeii during the Roman Republic, as the house takes up over three thousand square feet and covers an entire city block, also known as insulae.

Another important work of art found in the hidden riches of the House of the Faun was the *Alexander Mosaic*. The mosaic depicts the Battle of Issus (also known as the Battle of Issos), which took place in 333 BCE. This battle involved the forces of Alexander the Great and those of Darius III of Persia. The battle is notable for being one of Alexander the Great's earliest victories in his campaign to conquer Asia, and it was the first time he met Darius III in pitched battle. The *Alexander Mosaic* once decorated the floor of the House of the Faun; it was one of many floor mosaics that have been discovered in the estate. The work contains several different artistic influences, such as Hellenistic and Roman. Archaeologists believe that the mosaic was either copied from or inspired by the original painting of the battle, which was possibly painted by an Eritrean

painter named Philoxenus sometime in the 4th century BCE. The mosaic is notable for its depiction of fifty men (which was no small feat back then, considering the amount of work it took to arrange the tesserae, the colored tiles that make up a mosaic) and its attention to detail, especially considering it found its home in a private residence. Today, the original *Alexander Mosaic* is displayed at the Museo Archeologico Nazionale di Napoli (the National Archaeological Museum of Naples), although you can view a recreated copy at the House of the Faun, which is open to the public.

The original Alexander Mosaic from the House of the Faun, photographed in the National Archaeological Museum of Naples, 2008.

Magrippa at the English Wikipedia, CC BY-SA 3.0 <http://creativecommons.org/licenses/by-sa/3.0/>, via Wikimedia Commons
https://commons.wikimedia.org/wiki/File:Alexandermosaic.jpg

If you get the chance to visit the House of the Faun, you will notice that at the entrance to the three-thousand-square-foot house, there is a sign that says "HAVE," which was a variation of the Latin word *ave*, which was used as a salutation. When translated, *ave* is an imperative form of the verb *avēre*, which means "be well," and it was used as a greeting and to say goodbye to parting guests.

The "HAVE" inscription at the entrance of the House of the Faun.
Hibernian, CC BY-SA 3.0 <https://creativecommons.org/licenses/by-sa/3.0>, via Wikimedia Commons https://commons.wikimedia.org/wiki/File:HAVE_-_House_in_Pompeii.jpg

Among the preserved art pieces was an erotic mosaic of a satyr and a nymph, as well as one of a fish. A mosaic depicting theater masks, accompanied by fruit and flowers, was also discovered. The surviving art excavated from the volcanic residue reveals only a glimpse into the luxurious lifestyle the aristocratic Roman families in Pompeii enjoyed.

A Quick Look at How the Romans Incorporated Greek Culture
As you can see from the above examples, the Romans were fascinated by Greek culture, whether it be their art, philosophy, or even religion and religious motifs. By taking a look at the *Alexander Mosaic* found in the House of the Faun, we can find out more about

the Romans' inclination toward Greek art and motifs simply by examining the location and the position of the mosaic in the House of the Faun. The mosaic was located in the center of the visual axis between two peristyles, hinting that this art piece was a central decoration in the house. In fact, it would have been the first thing a visitor noticed when stepping into the room. By placing the artwork in such a noticeable spot, scholars presume that the Romans living there wanted to make sure their guests understood the kind of power their hosts wanted to emulate. So, even though Alexander the Great was Macedonian (the Macedonians were related to the Greeks, although there were some notable differences), the Romans chose him over a prominent Roman figure. The mosaic also features some classic Greek elements, with an emphasis being placed on the emotional expression of the fighters.

Another significant find reflecting the influence of Greek art on Roman culture is *The Three Graces*, a fresco that was discovered in the house of Titus Dentatus Panthera. The Graces were a part of Greek religion as minor goddesses, and they represented charm, beauty, goodwill, fertility, and human creativity. The fresco depicts the Three Graces naked, dancing in a circle and carrying myrtle while wearing wreaths. Although three was the typical number for the Graces in Greek myths, there could be more.

The Three Graces, found in the house of Titus Dentatus Panthera, created sometime

in the 1st century CE. A fresco located in the National Archaeological Museum of Naples (the Museo Archeologico Nazionale di Napoli).

One of the most popular art pieces that were inspired by Greek art that has been found in Pompeii was the *Doryphoros*.

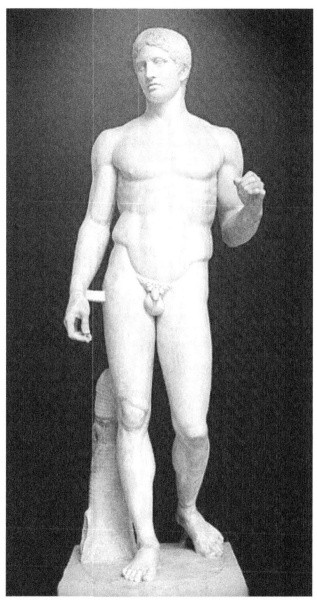

A preserved copy of the Roman Doryphoros. It is made of marble and stands almost seven feet high. Located today in the National Archaeological Museum of Naples.

The *Doryphoros* ("Spear-Bearer") was sculpted by Polykleitos, and it depicts a muscular warrior with a strong build. The statue originally had a spear that balanced on the soldier's left shoulder, hence the name of this art piece. The original statue, which was made of bronze, was lost sometime around 440 BCE (in fact, none of Polykleitos's works survived to the modern era). However, it inspired numerous marble copies, which were mostly made by the Romans.

The influence of this statue might lie in the fact that the *Doryphoros* was supposed to represent the perfectly balanced proportions of a young man, as Polykleitos designed it with the intention of showing what one can accomplish in the sculpted form. He created the sculpture so he could depict what he wrote in his "Canon," translated as "measure." Polykleitos's "Canon" was his vision of a man's perfect proportions.

The notable Greek doctor and writer Galen wrote about the

Doryphoros sometime in the 2nd century CE:

"Chrysippos [a Greek philosopher] holds beauty to consist not in the commensurability or 'symmetria' [i.e., proportions] of the constituent elements [of the body], but in the commensurability of the parts, such as that of finger to finger, and of all the fingers to the palm and wrist, and of those to the forearm, and of the forearm to the upper arm, and in fact, of everything to everything else, just as it is written in the Canon of Polyclitus. For having taught us in that work all the proportions of the body, Polyclitus supported his treatise with a work: he made a statue according to the tenets of his treatise, and called the statue, like the work, the 'Canon.'"

Unfortunately for scholars, Polykleitos's "Canon" has been lost in the sands of time. The marble copy that was found in Pompeii dates to sometime between 120 BCE to 50 BCE, and it stands at a whopping six feet eleven inches.

The House of the Tragic Poet

Greek writers greatly influenced Roman culture. The Romans were fascinated by Greek mythology, tragedies, stories, and legends.

Greek literature had an impact on Roman writing, and many of the classics of ancient Greece were translated from Greek to Latin. Modern scholars can thank the Romans for preserving many classics that were written by the ancient Greeks.

Greek literature was likewise depicted on murals and walls of wealthy homes in Pompeii. Perhaps the most valuable evidence of Pompeiians embracing Greek literature through art can be found in the House of the Tragic Poet, also known as the Homeric House or the Iliadic House.

This home was most likely built around the 2nd century BCE, like most of the surviving Pompeiian buildings. The house is famous for its detailed murals and mosaics, which depict scenes from Greek literature and Greek mythology. The house was discovered during the excavations that took place during the 1800s, and to the surprise of the archaeologists working on the site, the house revealed works of an artist who must have been a meticulous master of their time. They were, of course, inspired by Greek culture.

The size of the house does not imply that it belonged to a wealthy family; however, the number of discovered murals and mosaics and the quality of the work make scholars believe that this house indeed belonged to a noble family. As with many things of the ancient world, nothing is entirely for certain, and certainly nothing is known about the family or individual who lived in what we now refer to as the House of the Tragic Poet. It is likely the house belonged to someone who was wealthier, as archaeologists have confirmed that the house once had a second story.

The House of the Tragic Poet was originally the home to more than twenty painted mosaics and murals, many of which contained scenes from Homer's *Iliad* and *Odyssey*. The building also housed numerous scenes from Greek mythology, including a mural depicting Zeus, the god Hypnos (the god of sleep), and the goddess Hera on Mount Ida, also known as the Mountain of the Goddess, which is mentioned in the *Iliad*.

The Wedding of Zeus and Hera on Mount Ida, found in the House of the Tragic Poet, located today in the Museo Archaeological Nazionale di Napoli (the National Archaeology Museum of Naples).

The mural, now known as *The Wedding of Zeus and Hera on Mount Ida*, depicts Hypnos presenting Hera to Zeus, who is seated on a throne. At the bottom of the throne, the artist painted three male figures that might depict Dactyls. Dactyls are mythical creatures in

Greek mythology that represent male spirits and are associated with the cult of the Great Mother (either Cybele or Rhea, as both are seen as mother goddesses).

Another mural found in the House of the Tragic Poet that most likely referenced both the *Iliad* and Greek mythology depicts Aphrodite. The mural was almost completely destroyed when it was discovered, but it has been suggested that the part of the painting that is missing showed a seated man, most likely Paris. Aphrodite was painted as a smaller figure compared to other murals, so it is entirely possible there was more to the painting. Thus, scholars suggest that the mural depicted the Judgment of Paris, which is a scene from the *Iliad* that brought about the Trojan War due to Paris having to judge who was the most beautiful of the goddesses who claimed the golden apple.

Another scene from the *Iliad* found in the House of the Tragic Poet depicts Achilles as he gives up Briseis, who was given to Achilles as a prize of war. Achilles was furious that he had to give his prize up, and he refused to join the battle, although he did so once Patroclus was killed. The scene shows Achilles seated as he reluctantly gives up Briseis. Patroclus, who was most likely Achilles's lover and who was later avenged by Achilles on the battlefield, leads Briseis, holding her by the wrist and taking her to Agamemnon's messenger.

Achilles surrendering Briseis to Agamemnon, a fresco found in Pompeii and now located in the National Archaeological Museum of Naples, photographed by Sailko.
https://commons.wikimedia.org/wiki/File:Achille,_Patrocle,_Bris%C3%A9is_-

Yet another exceptional illustration of Greek literature and mythology can be found in the House of the Tragic Poet, that of Helen of Troy boarding the ship to sail back to her homeland. Although the mural was not entirely preserved, it is suggested that Paris was depicted, most likely already seated on the ship while waiting for Helen.

These examples are just a handful of what was found in the House of the Tragic Poet, as almost the entire home was decorated in marvelous, breathtaking paintings of scenes from Greek literature, showing the extent of the influence of Greek culture on Romans and their lifestyle.

Greek Theater

Greek drama was born with the Greek tragedy, and it soon became a popular form of art and entertainment across the Mediterranean and Rome. Ancient Greek theater dates back to the 6th century BCE and draws its roots from Athens, the cradle of Greek civilization. Greek theater was very much alive and popular in Pompeii as well, and the most valuable proof for that is found in the House of the Faun. The excavations of the House of the Faun revealed not only a private theater but also a mosaic with theatrical masks surrounded by flowers, fruit, and garlands.

Theatrical mask, mosaic found in the House of the Faun, Pompeii, author Marie-Lan Nguyen, 2011.

https://commons.wikimedia.org/wiki/File:Theatre_mask_mosaic_MAN_Napoli_Inv9994.jpg

However, the vast majority of the people of Pompeii enjoyed theater out in the open. In fact, Pompeii was home to two stone theaters before the first permanent theater was even opened in Rome. The largest theater in Pompeii was built sometime in the 2nd century BCE, and it could hold around five thousand people. It is believed that the theaters of Pompeii mostly held gladiator games, although dramas and concerts would have also taken place. The Amphitheatre of Pompeii has undergone many renovations over the years, and a restoration effort has taken place in recent years so it can once again be used for its original purpose: entertaining the masses.

Greek Religion

Greek religion also found its way to Pompeii and into the hearts of the Romans. One of the most important religious cults in Pompeii (and the Roman territories in general) was the cult of Apollo, who is the Greek god of archery, prophecy, music, dance, and poetry. The location of Pompeii's Temple of Apollo reveals its importance in the religious life of the people, as it was built in the center of the city in the Forum. The temple was built by the Romans to honor this ancient cult, which could be found across all of Magna Graecia (present-day Campania, Apulia, and Sicily, among other southern Italian regions), revealing the popularity of Apollo, who was one of the main deities in Rome.

The excavations of the Temple of Apollo have revealed that it was originally built in the 6th century BCE, making it one of the oldest religious buildings in Pompeii. However, it was rebuilt as the years passed. Sometime in the 2nd century BCE, the temple had been rebuilt (whether it was due to a natural disaster or not is unknown). The temple was once again updated after the massive earthquake that took place in 62 CE (it is believed this earthquake was a warning for what was to come later on in 79 CE). The temple was not entirely reconstructed by the time of the fateful eruption of Mount Vesuvius, though.

The Temple of Apollo, Pompeii.
Lord Pheasant at en.wikipediaLord Pheasant, CC BY-SA 3.0
<https://creativecommons.org/licenses/by-sa/3.0>, via Wikimedia Commons
https://commons.wikimedia.org/wiki/File:Pompeii_-_Temple_of_Apollo_1400px.png

Temples were the center of religious life for the Pompeiians. However, the people of Pompeii did not solely practice their faith by visiting temples. Mystery cults and festivals were also some of the ways they expressed gratitude to the gods, whether they were Greek, Roman, or foreign.

Another popular cult was that of Dionysus, the god of wine and fertility. The Romans worshiped Dionysus under a different name, though. They referred to him as Bacchus, which again shows signs of the Latinization of foreign cultures and religions. The Romans would keep spiritual motifs from other religions but would often name the gods differently compared to the source religion. Some well-known examples are Jupiter (the Greek Zeus) and Neptune (the Greek Poseidon).

Until 186 BCE, festivities were organized by the cult of Bacchus to celebrate the god of wine and fertility. These festivities were known as Bacchanalia, and according to the Roman historian Livy, these festivals included sexual promiscuity and endless rivers of alcohol, which, predictably, caused aggressive behavior and festive chaos in the streets of Rome and Roman provinces. Most likely because the cult negatively affected public and political life across the Roman territories, the festivities were outlawed along with the cult in 186 BCE by the Roman Senate. However, while Bacchanalias became a thing of the past in Rome, these festivities were still celebrated in Pompeii and Campania, and its people kept the cult of Dionysus very much alive.

The Villa of the Mysteries

If one wants to understand the importance and the popularity of the mystery cults, one needs to look no further than the well-preserved suburban villa known as the Villa of the Mysteries. The Villa of the Mysteries is home to some of the most beautiful frescos found so far in the excavations of Pompeii. A single room in the Villa of the Mysteries contained a whole series of frescos that are thought to depict the initiation of a woman into a mystery cult. The frescos were discovered in 1909, but they were badly damaged due to poor protection from the elements and an earthquake that rocked the area a few months after the villa was discovered.

One of the frescos, depicting the reading of rituals for a mystery cult found in the Villa of the Mysteries, Pompeii, The Yorck Project, 2002.

The series of frescos was most likely created between 70 BCE and 60 BCE, and many historians believe that the series depicts a woman being initiated into the cult of Dionysus, although the subject of the series is still being debated today. One of the main clues that indicate the painting was about the cult of Dionysius (or the cult of Bacchus) is what appears to be the depiction of maenads, the female followers of Dionysius.

For those unfamiliar with mystery cults, they were characterized by the use of secrecy. It is believed the cult worshipers were carefully selected. Once chosen, they would partake in an initiation ritual and be sworn to keep the cult's secrets, which included their practices; thus, historians have to rely on other sources to learn more about the mystery cults, sources that may be biased against them. For instance, Justin Martyr, a Christian writer, referred to mystery cults as "demonic imitations."

The fifth fresco, depicting a rite in honor of Bacchus, the Villa of the Mysteries,
Pompeii, The Yorck Project, 2002.

The House of the Garden of Hercules and the House of the

Vettii

The Romans also worshiped Heracles, the son of Zeus, only under a different name, Hercules. The Romans regarded the Greek demigod as the ultimate hero, as he was renowned for his strength and might. According to the Romans and the Latinized myth of Heracles, Hercules was the son of Jupiter, the Roman equivalent of Zeus, who was famous and worshiped for his many adventures. The House of the Garden of Hercules and the House of the Vettii have survived as testaments of the importance and significance of the cult of Hercules in Pompeii.

In the House of the Garden of Hercules, a statue of Hercules was found along with a shrine and an altar dedicated to the cult. (The home was also known for its garden; pollen analyses indicate that roses, lilies, and violets were once grown there.)

More evidence of the cult of Hercules was revealed in the reception room in the House of the Vettii, which was one of the largest homes in Pompeii. Many frescos were discovered in the home, including a mural depicting a mythological scene in which baby Hercules strangles the snake that Hera sent to kill him after she found out about Zeus's affair with Alcmene (also known as Alcmena), Hercules's mother.

Hercules as an infant, strangling a snake, the House of the Vettii, Pompeii.
AlMare Attribution-ShareAlike 2.5 Generic (CC BY-SA 2.5).
https://creativecommons.org/licenses/by-sa/2.5/deed.en via Wikimedia Commons,
*https://upload.wikimedia.org/wikipedia/commons/b/bc/Pompeji_Casa_Dei_Vettii_Hercules_*
Child_Detail.jpg

Remains of Egyptian Culture in Pompeii

Pompeii was influenced by Egyptian culture to some extent since

Rome and Egypt shared political interests during the early 2nd century BCE. However, Rome was not truly influenced by Egypt until the conflicts between Octavian Augustus and Mark Antony and Cleopatra ensued. As a result of being subdued by the Romans in 30 BCE, Egypt started to send new riches and materials to Rome, such as papyrus, glass, and various ores. Due to these new goods coming from Egypt, the Romans became fascinated by the Egyptian culture, which resulted in the Romans embracing Egyptian art, architecture, and even religion. This influence was present in Pompeii as well.

The remarkable House of the Faun testifies to this fascination with Egyptian art and culture, as archaeologists have discovered a table stand in the form of a sphinx, as well as a magnificent mosaic depicting the Nile River and its fascinating flora and fauna, including crocodiles, ibis, and hippopotamus. The Sphinx was a decorative motif that the Pompeiians embraced, as it was discovered in various public and private establishments around the city, providing a glimpse into the widespread acceptance of the Egyptian culture and mythology among the people of Pompeii.

The House of Julia Felix

The House of Julia Felix, a large property in Pompeii, was home to an impressive peristyle thought to represent a branch of the Nile Delta. The garden also has a series of connected water channels and marble walkaways, and it is decorated with tall, elegant columns and statues.

The House of Julia Felix was named after its owner, a woman who is said to have owned the building and the property surrounding it. Although Julia Felix was a public figure in Pompeii, it is likely she was an illegitimate daughter, as an inscription states she was the "low-born, illegitimate daughter of Spurius," meaning she was born out of wedlock. However, not all historians agree, as other scholars believe that Julia descended from freedmen.

It is not known for certain how Julia Felix got her hands on the house, but it is known that she rented it out as apartments or some kind of living unit after the 62 CE earthquake. Owning land as a woman was somewhat disputable during Julia's lifetime (it is not known when she lived, but she was alive in 62 CE, which means she might have been alive when Mount Vesuvius erupted in 79 CE). During that time, women were not allowed to legally own property without a male guardian of some kind, whether that be a father or a husband, unless she wanted to jump through many hoops (however, if a woman was of noble birth, she would not have faced as many challenges as those of lower stations did). Some women were allowed to own property if they were independent of their male guardian, which appears to have been the case with Julia Felix.

The Temple of Isis

Egyptian culture can be traced to religious cults in Pompeii as well. Aside from worshiping Graeco-Roman gods and goddesses, the people of Pompeii seem to have grown fond of Egyptian deities, as they celebrated Anubis (god of the afterlife), Bes (god of childbirth and fertility), and Isis (goddess of the rain, although she held many other roles).

The cult of Isis was one of the many mystery cults that sprang up in the area, and it was important to the city judging by the Temple of Isis, which was erected in the same district where the theater and gymnasium were built. Historians think the cult first made an appearance in Pompeii around 100 BCE, with it most likely being introduced by the Greeks due to their acceptance and admiration of Egyptian culture, and it gained traction due to its popularity with slaves, freedmen, and women. The cult later found a following with noblemen. It is thought the cult of Isis was so attractive to such a wide audience due to the people's belief that Isis could grant immortality. According to Egyptian mythology, Isis raised her own husband, Osiris (god of the dead), from the dead after he was killed by his brother Set (god of disorder and violence).

The Temple of Isis, Pompeii, author Juliana Bastos Marques.

The temple was destroyed in an earthquake in 62 CE. However, the temple was soon rebuilt, which shows how popular the cult of Isis was in Pompeii. In fact, it was the only temple that was completely rebuilt after being damaged by the earthquake before the eruption of Mount Vesuvius in 79 CE.

At the Temple of Isis, priests would engage in daily rituals. Twice a day, priests would hold ceremonies, with the first ceremony starting before sunrise, which symbolically celebrated the re-birth of Osiris, Isis's husband. During the second ceremony, which took place in the afternoon, the priests would bless water that had been taken from the Nile to acknowledge their gratitude to Isis.

The paintings found in the Temple of Isis were done in the

Hellenistic style, which was likely done to ensure the people accepted her into Roman culture. One fresco depicts a priest wearing the mask of Anubis, a god who was often shown having the head of a black jackal.

Anubis is believed to be one of the oldest gods among Egyptian deities since he was the god of the dead. Anubis is related to the afterlife and mummification in Egyptian religion, but he was accepted as a god and worshiped by the Romans in Pompeii. More evidence of the worship of Anubis was found in the House of the Golden Cupids (named for the Cupids found on the portico, a roofed structure that attaches the porch to the building). The House of the Golden Cupids is an amazing look into how much the Pompeiians revered Egyptian deities, as the house contains a shrine dedicated solely to them; it is possible that the owner was a priest in the cult of Isis due to the many objects in the house that pertained to her.

Anubis is depicted in the shrine as a man with a canine hand, which is typical for his portrayal in paintings, but there is also a detail that is not seen in Egyptian artwork, at least before the Greeks began to influence them. In the shrine, Anubis is seen holding a caduceus, which is a staff characteristic for the Greek god Hermes (or the Roman god Mercury, which would have been the case in Pompeii). This combination of the two gods resulted in a god with the name of Hermanubis, and he signified the Egyptian priesthood.

Portrayals of Bes, the god of sexuality, music, humor, and childbirth, to name a few attributes, were also present in Pompeii. Bes was often depicted as a dwarf with monstrous features, such as large eyes, oversized ears, bowlegs, and exaggerated genitals. In the Temple of Isis, a portrayal of Bes is found in the Sacrarium, which is a small shrine that could be located in either a public or private sanctuary.

As an interesting side note, the Temple of Isis influenced the art world almost a full century later when thirteen-year-old Wolfgang Amadeus Mozart visited the temple. His visit later gave him the inspiration to write *The Magic Flute*, a well-received opera that premiered shortly before his death.

Chapter 4 – The Romans in Pompeii: Life in Pompeii under Rome

Rome's influence on Pompeii began during the Samnite period. As mentioned above, the Romans finally subdued the Samnites in 290 BCE, and with the Samnites' submission came their territories, which included Pompeii. Although Pompeii was certainly in the Roman sphere of influence, it was, for the most part, left to its own devices. That changed about two hundred years after the Samnites were subdued, as the Pompeiians wanted more out of their arrangement with Rome.

The Social Wars, which lasted from 91 BCE to 87 BCE, was briefly touched on in a previous chapter, but it had significant ramifications for Pompeii and other cities in Campania, so it is essential we take a closer look at them. During these conflicts, the Roman Republic once again had to reinstate its dominance in Italy, for Italian cities, which had been a part of the Roman territory for centuries, started to rebel against Rome. The match that ignited the flames of the Social Wars was a request for Roman citizenship. Although these Italic tribes and cities were allies of Rome and technically a part of the Roman Republic, they did not have the same rights as those who lived in Rome. The people of these Italian cities wanted to have all the privileges and rights that came with Roman citizenship, namely the right to vote. By having the right to vote, the people could have a say in who represented them in the Senate. They could choose people who had their best interests at heart, someone who could help fight against the land and wealth inequality that the people had been facing for many years. The people of these Italian cities knew they aided Rome by sending soldiers, yet they did not see any benefits to this, as most of the land remained in Roman hands while their men faced the chance of dying in war. As the Greek historian Appian put it, the "Italic people [were] declining little by little into pauperism and paucity of numbers without any hope of remedy." The people of these cities also knew that Roman citizenship and the right to vote would grant them more influence, both within their city and in Rome itself, allowing them to further increase their status.

Since these cities had been a part of the Roman Republic for over two hundred years, they felt Roman citizenship was the least Rome could offer them for staying so loyal. While these cities were independent, at least in terms of governance, they could still owe tribute to Rome, and they did send Rome many soldiers; it is estimated that between one-half and two-thirds of the soldiers in the Roman army came from these Italian cities. The people just wanted Rome to treat them equally as "children of the Republic," but Rome did not want to hear about it. What Rome did not know was that another war was about to break out.

In 91 BCE, Marcus Livius Drusus championed the cause of the Italian cities. However, he was assassinated before making any real headway, inflaming the people's passions and leading them to believe they had no other choice but war. The Social Wars involved many Italic tribes, such as the Marsi and the Samnites, but other people groups, such as the Latins and the Etruscans, refused to get involved, with the Latins actively remaining loyal to the Romans while the Etruscans just remained neutral (they were later granted Roman citizenship to keep them from entering the war). It is possible they stayed out of the war because they feared what would happen to them in case the rebels' efforts were thwarted by the mighty Roman Republic. The Pompeiians were some of those who battled against Roman rule, and they remained in the fight for two years.

The rebels sought not only to separate from Rome but also to create their own confederation, which would, hopefully in time, rival that of Rome. Of course, this never came to fruition. The rebels certainly put up a good fight, though, especially in the first year of the conflict. By 89 BCE, the tides had turned. Lucius Cornelius Sulla, better known simply as Sulla, was a gifted general, and he, along with Gaius Marius, another brilliant commander, led the charge. Sulla overtook the city of Pompeii, causing the people to finally wave the white flag, but they were not alone. Since most of the rebel leaders had been killed, the war was essentially over (except for the Samnites in the south), although the resistance carried on in small pockets of Italy.

Though the Samnites were still a fairly large threat to the Romans, Rome began granting Roman citizenship to those Italian cities who had rebelled but surrendered under a new law called the *Lex Plautia Papiria de Civitate Sociis Danda*. It was a smart move on Rome's part; it gave the people what they had wanted, ensuring that more cities would surrender. Although the formation of a confederation would be off the table, the people could now vote or run for public office. The Samnites held out until the bitter end, and when the Social Wars began to morph into a different civil war, that of Sulla's civil war, the Samnites continued their fight against the general. Sulla won that war as well, and the Greek historian Strabo stated that some of the Samnites' cities "dwindled into villages, some indeed being entirely deserted."

The end of the Social Wars, as well as the end of Sulla's civil war, resulted in the complete Romanization of the Italian cities, which began to fully embrace the Roman way of life. As a result, they were slowly stripped of their cultural and linguistic identities through natural and political assimilation. Rome had finally established its complete hegemony over the Italian Peninsula, which included the city of Pompeii.

After the Social Wars ended, Pompeii became a Roman colony named Colonia Cornelia Veneria Pompeianorum. Although much of the land in Pompeii went to Sulla's veterans and although those who had supported the Social Wars had their property stripped from them, the Pompeiians quickly adapted to Roman citizenship, even adopting Latin as their main language. And the city rapidly became a jewel in the crown of Rome, thanks to its favorable geographic position, fertile lands, and great potential for economic growth.

Pompeii had always been a leading city in Campania when it came to maritime and trading activities, and its riches had helped merchants and entrepreneurs establish themselves in the city and reap the many benefits that Roman citizenship offered them. Merchants become so rich that they even competed with noble families in building the grandest villa! This new "middle class" probably bothered the nobility somewhat, as the nobles had a standard to keep when it came to splendor. Traditionally, this power and influence had always belonged to the nobility, and the newly rich middle class enjoyed outdoing the nobles by building marvelous villas and gardens with flower beds, fountains, pools, and statues. The middle class showed off their wealth through ornaments and jewelry as well, which had also been only characteristic of the aristocracy.

Although Pompeii had been one of the wealthiest cities in Campania for hundreds of years, the Romans wanted to place an even larger emphasis on its riches and its desirability, which caused people to flock there in droves. And who could blame them? Wealth, riches, and prosperity call to everyone. Scenic views, rich farmland, and the thought of accumulating more wealth were enough to make the noblemen of Rome move to Pompeii and call it their home, erecting astonishing villas and commissioning artists to create masterpieces of antiquity, some of which managed to stay preserved under the volcanic ash.

In general, the standard of living significantly improved across all social classes. One sign of the burgeoning wealth in Pompeii was the Via dell'Abbondanza, one of the main streets in Pompeii. The Via dell'Abbondanza was actually the longest street in Pompeii, sitting at around nine hundred meters (almost three thousand feet). It had an intersection with the Forum, which was the center of daily life. At the intersection with the Forum sat two major public buildings: the Eumachia building (it is unknown what the purpose of this building was; it is possible it was a marketplace or used as a guild's headquarters) and the Comitum (the polling place). Near the Forum,

Romans could pay tribute to some of the main deities they shared with the Hellenic culture, as they could visit the temple of Apollo, Venus (known to the Greeks as Aphrodite), or Jupiter (the Greek god Zeus).

The Via dell'Abbondanza translates to the "Street of Abundance," and it is easy to see why. As one of the main streets of Pompeii, it was naturally one of the most crowded streets, packed to the brim with shops, workshops, bars, bakeries, and restaurants. It was a busy, colorful street that perhaps demonstrates the life and wealth of the city. The street also had a large public bath, and its crossroads led to many important establishments, such as the theaters.

Like other Roman cities, Pompeii had an aqueduct system that supplied the city with water, which was used for public baths and fountains. Wealthy Pompeiians even had running water in the comfort of their splendid villas. Instead of a modern-day toilet, they used a wooden seat that was built over a pit. After disposing of their waste, they would flush it away with a bucket of water, which then drained into either a cesspool beneath the street or close to the house. Although much of Pompeii was preserved, the aqueduct was one of the features that were not.

The view on the coast was breathtaking, which was perhaps one of the many reasons aristocrats from Rome were drawn to Pompeii. Summer homes adorned Pompeii's coastline, which overlooked the nearby Bay of Naples. Since the city was built 40 meters above sea level (around 131 feet) on a plateau created by previous eruptions of Mount Vesuvius, the view of the landscape was perhaps unparalleled to any other city in Campania except nearby Herculaneum, to some extent. One such summer villa was Oplontis, which is believed to have been owned by Poppaea Sabina the Younger, Emperor Nero's second wife, although scholars are still unsure if it truly belonged to her.

The front garden of the Villa Poppaea, photo by Miguel Hermoso Cuesta.

Although many wealthy Romans and noble families were able to take advantage of summer homes by the water on those hot sunny days, not everyone could. Like other major cities, Pompeii was home to plenty of poor people. Antonio Varone, who was once the director of the excavations at Pompeii, said, "There was an extraordinarily well-off class that really enjoyed itself. From the excavations we have seen that there was a huge part of the population that lived in poverty, that struggled with daily life." It is believed around ten thousand to twenty thousand people lived in Pompeii, while some estimations suggest that fifteen thousand inhabitants is a somewhat more accurate number.

The people of Pompeii enjoyed their entertainment, which went hand in hand with the splendor and wealth of the city. They could visit a massive amphitheater that had the capacity to seat perhaps up to twenty thousand people, although it is more likely that the amphitheater sat closer to twelve thousand people. There, the people could watch gladiator games, which was a tradition derived from Roman culture. These were free to watch, and Varone hypothesizes that "the masses were helped in this way, [as] the powerful wanted them to remain tranquil."

Aside from the large amphitheater, there were several public and private theaters that hosted musical concerts, plays, and religious festivities. The theater area in Pompeii, with the large amphitheater as the centerpiece, also had the Odeon and Quadriporticum. The Odeon was a smaller theater; it is believed it could have seated around 1,500 people. The other major structure in the theater area, the Quadriporticum, was a covered walkway behind the theater, which allowed the people to travel to their destination without getting rained on. During the Roman Empire, these theaters were almost completely repurposed for gladiator games.

Inside of the Amphitheatre of Pompeii, Buckeye~commonswiki assumed (based on copyright claims).

The Amphitheatre of Pompeii was built around 70 BCE, and, as mentioned above, it is the oldest preserved Roman amphitheater made of stone, preceding the Colosseum in Rome by an entire century (it should be noted that stone theaters were built in Rome before the establishment of the Colosseum, but the one in Pompeii still predates those). Previously, the Romans built their amphitheaters from wood. The term *amphitheatrum*, from which we derive our modern-day term of "amphitheater," was not in use when the Amphitheatre of Pompeii was built. Instead, Romans called it the *spectacula*. The amphitheater was so modern for its time that it even had a washroom in a nearby palestra, which also housed a gymnasium where wrestlers and boxers could practice.

The Amphitheatre of Pompeii was also the site where a major confrontation occurred between the people of Pompeii and the Nucerians (a city near Naples) in 59 CE, a little over a half-century after the Social Wars broke out in the Italian Peninsula. The Roman historian Tacitus wrote the following passage about the brawl:

"About this time [59 CE] there was a serious fight between the inhabitants of two Roman settlements, Nuceria and Pompeii. It arose out of a trifling incident at a gladiatorial show…During an exchange of taunts—characteristic of these disorderly country towns —abuse led to stone-throwing, and then swords were drawn. The people of Pompeii, where the show was held, came off best. Many wounded and mutilated Nucerians were taken to the capital. Many bereavements, too, were suffered by parents and children. The emperor [Nero] instructed the senate to investigate the affair. The senate passed it to the consuls. When they reported back, the senate debarred Pompeii from holding any similar gathering for ten years. Illegal associations in the town were dissolved; and the sponsor of the show and his fellow-instigators of the disorders were exiled."

The Amphitheatre of Pompeii, detail from a larger fresco, National Archaeological Museum of Naples, U.D.F., Paris - Robert Etienne: Pompeii, die eingeäscherte Stadt, Ravensburg 1991.

The games most likely did not incite the violent confrontation that day. Back during the Social Wars, Nuceria was one of the cities that did not rebel against the Roman Republic. It is likely they held a grudge against the Pompeiians, who received the same benefits as they did even though they rebelled against Rome. This dormant hostility was awoken around two years before the riot took place when Emperor Nero placed a group of veterans in Nuceria. It is even possible that the Pompeiians believed those lands belonged to them, which would make tensions more hostile between the two.

While Emperor Nero and the Roman Senate concluded that the Amphitheatre of Pompeii should not host gladiatorial games for ten years, it is quite probable the ban was not fully enforced. Evidence found during the excavations suggests that the amphitheater was still serving its purpose during the ten-year ban, most likely because of Nero's second wife, Poppaea Sabina the Younger, who was born in Pompeii. She might have intervened with this decision as her mother's family still lived in Pompeii (it is also possible Poppaea herself had a summer home there). At the very least, beast hunts and athletic competitions still took place during the ban.

In 62 CE, only a couple of years after the incident, a major earthquake devastated the city of Pompeii and Herculaneum, and the Amphitheatre of Pompeii was damaged along with many other buildings. Even buildings in Naples and Nuceria suffered damage, although not nearly to the extent in Pompeii. The earthquake was, in reality, a warning to what was about to happen to the entire city of Pompeii seventeen years later. Another minor earthquake was felt two years later, in 64 CE. Although some of the city was rebuilt by the time of the eruption, a good chunk of it was still damaged. The Amphitheatre of Pompeii was one of the buildings that were repaired before the volcano erupted, and as a way to placate the people who had suffered so much, it was quickly reopened to the public.

The Roman Republic ruled a large portion of the Mediterranean and had established its dominance in other territories as well, such as Africa and western Asia. The Roman Republic was essentially an empire before it officially became one. During the years of wars and battles, the Romans enjoyed art, played games, and even practiced the modern-day concept of "summer vacation." And Pompeii might be the perfect example of the splendor and wealth that now characterizes Rome.

In 27 BCE, the Roman Republic officially became the Roman

Empire, with Rome as its only capital. Long before the Roman Empire would come to an end in 476 CE, which coincides with the beginning of the Middle Ages and the massive adoption of Christianity, Pompeii would have already found its demise in the ashes of Mount Vesuvius.

Chapter 5 – Daily Life of the People of Pompeii

Daily life in Pompeii can be traced back many hundreds of years, for the eruption that took the lives of all the citizens essentially froze the city in time, preserving evidence that can provide a clearer insight into how the people of Pompeii went about their daily lives and routines.

Although wars and conflicts were a constant occurrence ever since Pompeii was founded by the Oscans to the day it was colonized by the Roman Republic, the Pompeiians' daily life, for the most part, was far from stressful and mostly consisted of simple and mundane activities that created nearly carefree routines. It might be hard to imagine a time when street lights and electricity were not around, as they are such a constant part of our lives today. However, we have to go back to a time where people would rise early in the morning with the first signs of the sun.

In the period between four and six in the morning, which was known as *hora prima diurna* ("hour before daytime"), people would rise to go to work. The first thing they would do was fetch water from the public fountains, which were accessible to everyone in the city. Only the richest and the wealthiest had running water in their homes. Over time, the Romans placed great emphasis on their hygiene. Water was important, as the Romans used it for bathing, washing, and drinking.

Initially, the Romans were a fairly dirty bunch, especially by today's standards. Thanks to the Gauls, the Romans discovered a milder form of soap. The Gauls, however, used this soap to dye their hair, and men actually used it more often than the women. As time passed, the Romans began placing a greater emphasis on hygiene, utilizing the soap they had discovered from the Gauls. Bathing was extremely important in self-care. Unlike in many parts of the world today, bathing was often a public affair, so citizens would visit public baths to rinse the grime from their bodies. Of course, as we know today, this practice is incredibly unhygienic. Unless one replenishes the water in the public baths with fresh water, bacteria is sure to grow. But even though the Romans did not understand the concept of bacteria, they knew that bad water could cause one to have poor health. Archaeologists have even discovered several tombstones that state, "Baths, wine, and sex corrupt our bodies, but baths, wine, and sex make life worth living." Of course, those lucky enough to be rich could enjoy the comfort of private baths, meaning they did not have to fear the spreading of disease like others.

Just as it is today, breakfast was an important part of the morning. For breakfast, Pompeiians would typically eat cheese and bread, although they would sometimes have fruit or vegetables on the side. One of the earliest shops to open were barbershops, which usually opened at sunrise. At barbershops, the people would get their hair trimmed; barbers would also remove stray hairs and warts and clean nails, which included cutting the corns from people's feet. In ancient Rome, barbershops were more than just a place to ensure one looked good. People would flock to these establishments to relax and chat with others. Barbershops were a good place for getting the latest news and gossip, so these places were often packed with people.

Hora secunda ("second hour") lasted from six to seven in the morning. During this time, everyone would go about their work, whether they were slaves or merchants. All the shops were open by this point, not just the barbershops. Markets were also open for business, ready for those early visitors, and farmers were out in the field, going about their business before it got too hot.

At *Hora quarta* ("fourth hour"), which would be around eight to ten in the morning, there were more people out and about. They could be visiting shops and markets, or perhaps they were taking a stroll in the Forum, which would have certainly been teeming with life by this hour. At the Forum, people gathered to discuss problems, whether they be personal or related to the city itself, as well as chat with others about mundane and private things. By going to the Forum, one was able to connect with other citizens and find out if there might be any novelties in town or even gossip about a neighbor, a nobleman, or a politician.

Hora septima ("seventh hour") was the time of the day between noon and one in the afternoon. This time was reserved for relaxing and taking a break; it was essentially a siesta, as the weather can be very hot in Italy, and taking a break allowed the people to avoid working during the hottest part of the day. If Pompeiians decided to use their break to eat, and if they could afford it, they would often snack on fish, cake, bread, and fruit (the topic of food will be discussed in more detail below). At times, the aristocracy of the city would organize gladiator games, in which case people would head to the Amphitheatre of Pompeii. It may be hard for us to imagine that someone would enjoy a cruel fight between gladiators, considering the violence and gore that took place, but for the people of antiquity, gladiator games were entertaining. Spectators would have their favorites, and they would cheer for their champion and even quarrel with other spectators when they hooted for their champion's opponent, similar to the way people enjoy watching football games and have their favorite teams, the extreme blood and gore excluded. During *Hora Octava* ("eighth hour"), which lasted from about one to two in the afternoon, the Romans used thermal baths. Although the baths could be dirty, people still flocked there, not just to bathe but also to socialize. Even slaves who were third-class citizens with few rights could enjoy the public thermal baths. In fact, there were three entrances to the baths—women, men, and slaves. Eventually, mixed bathing became the norm.

There were at least five public thermal bath complexes in the city of Pompeii, where citizens could exercise, sweat, and then take a dip afterward. One could also purchase food or perfume, stop by the library to read a book, and even enjoy a musical performance. Not all of this would be located in the bathhouse itself (sometimes, it would be located adjacent to the building), and not every bathhouse contained such extravagant amenities. Thermal baths were also places where business and politics were talked about, where gossip was shared and the latest scandals revealed. As you can see, bathing was not just a mundane activity for the Romans; it was a well-ingrained routine and a way to practice a well-known maxim, *mens sana in corpore sano*, which translated from Latin means "a healthy mind in a healthy body," a phrase that refers to both bathing and physical exercise.

Speaking of health, it is thought the Romans had an average lifespan of twenty-five to thirty-five years. However, infant mortality was high back then, which considerably drops the average life expectancy. It is thought that around half of the Roman populace did not live past the age of five. So, if one was to factor the high infant mortality rate out, the average Roman would live to around fifty, maybe even late fifties.

At around two in the afternoon, the Romans would partake of their largest meal of the day (*cena*). As with many other aspects of Roman culture, the *cena* evolved as time passed. For instance, the Romans initially ate both the *cena* and the *vesperna*, a lighter meal at night. However, in time, the *cena* grew to become such an important and social affair that it replaced the *vesperna* entirely. The poor typically ate porridge and had vegetables or fruit on the side when possible. The wealthy, of course, ate much finer fare. They would dine on eggs, cheese, and sometimes even some kind of meat.

At *Hora Decima* ("tenth hour"), which would be around the time between four and five p.m., the people of Pompeii would have already been active for twelve hours of the day, and as the sun was slowly setting, citizens would leave their workplaces, markets, and shops and head home. Nighttime was a dangerous time of the day in Rome, so it is believed the same would have been true of Pompeii. After all, there were no street lights, and the only good source of light would have been the moon if the weather allowed for it. The thousands of oil lamps discovered in the excavations could hardly mitigate the darkness of gloomy nights. On top of this, alleys and streets were narrow and twisting. And there was also the chance of having someone throw their waste upon you since the darkness would have obscured your form. The Roman poet Decimus Junius Juvenalis, better known simply as Juvenal, touched upon this:

"And now think of the different and diverse perils of the night. See what a height it is to that towering roof from which a pot comes crack upon my head every time that some broken or leaky vessel is pitched out of the window! See with what a smash it strikes and dints the pavement! There's death in every open window as you pass along at night; you may well be deemed a fool, improvident of sudden accident, if you go out to dinner without having made your will…Yet however reckless the fellow may be, however hot with wine and young blood, he gives a wide berth to one whose scarlet cloak and long retinue of attendants, with torches and brass lamps in their hands, bid him keep his distance. But to me, who am wont to be escorted home by the moon, or by the scant light of a candle he pays no respect."

A popular nighttime activity for those who dared to stay out on the streets of Pompeii was writing graffiti on the walls of the city. One of the many wall inscriptions discovered in the city was signed by "the late drinkers," which testifies that life in Pompeii still went on during the evening and nighttime hours.

Over eleven thousand instances of graffiti were found in Pompeii alone. Graffiti was used for many purposes, such as advertisements for gladiator shows, businesses, warnings, and even personal messages. A good number of the preserved wall graffiti talks about inappropriate and bawdy subjects. For instance, outside the gladiators' barracks, archaeologists found graffiti that read, "Celadus the Thracian makes the girls moan!" (And that is a tamer example, believe it or not!) Some graffiti testify unrequited love, like the one that reads, "Successus the weaver's in love with Iris and she doesn't give a toss," painting both a colorful and mundane picture of life in the city.

Before going to bed, people would have their dinner, which, if one was poorer, usually consisted of olives and chicken eggs. Those who could afford it would possibly add meat, fish, or cake to their supper, going to bed with full stomachs.

The Romans were a busy people, and they did not always have time to go home and prepare a meal. Instead, and it might sound crazy to some of us today, they relied on fast food to get them through the day. Of course, their concept of fast food is different than ours, but there are similarities. It is believed the city of Pompeii had at least two hundred dining establishments, which would equate to one café for every sixty citizens. At these cafés, people would buy cheap hot food that was sold in jars. These cafés also sold wine, which the owners stacked behind the counter, which was typically long and stretched along the street to catch the eye of passersby. Oftentimes there was a room with tables and chairs in a room behind the counter, where people could sit while they grabbed a quick bite to eat and giving them yet another chance to socialize with their neighbors. The rich and wealthy would usually eat at home, where they had slaves and servants to accommodate them at their dining table in the privacy of their magnificent homes and villas. The poor lived in tiny rooms and often had no other option but to eat out since they did not have the facilities or time to prepare their food.

Although it sounds like the average Pompeiian did not have much food available to them, most Pompeiians had a rather healthy diet, even when buying cheap café food. This is known due to the seven hundred bags of waste that were collected from the sewers in the nearby city of Herculaneum. By examining the remains, scientists have discovered that these people ate fish and chicken, food normally reserved for the wealthy. Even the bodies of the poorer citizens that have been discovered show no signs of malnutrition, meaning the food they ate was most likely somewhat similar to what the nobles ate.

Since the region was perfect for farming, many different fruit and vegetables were cultivated. One of the most praised was cabbage. Cato the Elder (234–149 BCE) wrote about his love for cabbage and its beneficial impact on digestion. He also interestingly believed that if a person was sick, they should eat a lot of cabbage and then bathe in their urine so the sickness could leave their body faster. To give some credit to Cato, cabbage is incredibly healthy, as it is packed with vitamins and antioxidants. And although there are groups of people today who bathe in urine, no scientific evidence thus far has pointed out any positive benefits of doing so. The Romans also ate other vegetables, namely peas, rutabaga, artichokes, and brussels sprouts. However, these are not the same versions as we know them today; the modern-day versions of these veggies only began to be cultivated during the late Middle Ages.

Meat from a butcher's shop was incredibly rare, although the most popular meat was pork. Everyone but the extremely poor could afford pork as it was cheap, and since it was salted, it could last long without spoiling while traveling from the farms to the city. Beef was practically nonexistent, although the Greeks dined upon it. The Pompeiians would have also eaten wild game, mainly ducks and geese. However, fish was more likely to be on the table for meals, along with cheese. Slaves even ate seafood, although what they ate was mollusks (the people from Naples referred to mollusks as the mussels of the slaves). The rich people of Pompeii loved buying extravagant meat to show off their wealth. There have been reports of Romans eating flamingos and even giraffes! Of course, this was still incredibly rare. Another interesting delicacy that the wealthy ate was dormice. At dinner parties, they would even bring out the dead dormice to weigh in front of their guests to flaunt their wealth even more.

The most common fruit eaten in Pompeii were apples, pears,

pomegranates, figs, blackberries, dates, and grapes. Fruit was often eaten as an appetizer or dessert. Figs and dates were perhaps the most popular fruit among the wealthy. For instance, the dates could be stuffed with walnuts, pine nuts, and pepper, after which they were salted and then fried in honey. Olives and nuts were also an important part of the Pompeiians' diet, and wine would typically accompany a meal.

But without a doubt, bread was the most important staple in Pompeii. Both rich and poor alike ate bread, and the bread they ate did not really differ based on wealth. It was one of the few food items that crossed the social divide. Eighty-one carbonized loaves of bread have been found throughout the thirty-four bakeries that have so far been discovered.

The food the Pompeiians ate was not plain at all. According to archaeologists, the people of Pompeii had access to homegrown as well as exotic herbs and spices, which allowed them to enjoy both traditional and spicy dishes. Most families that had more than one room would also have a homegrown garden where they would cultivate, on a small scale, fresh herbs, spices, and some vegetables and fruit for personal use. Over time, these gardens transformed into massive gardens that displayed their wealth.

There was rarely a dish in Pompeii, as well as Rome, that did not use fish oil or the fermented fish sauce known as garum. There was also at least one shop in Pompeii that made and sold this smelly and, at least perhaps to us, repulsing concoction that consisted of rotten fish. One of the richest families in Pompeii actually made their fortune through solely trading garum. This is known due to their house, as their entrance hall was decorated with garum jars. Garum merchants knew how to expand their business, for they even produced kosher garum that contained no shellfish so they could sell garum to a local community of Jews that lived in Pompeii.

Most of the people from Pompeii were not wealthy from selling garum. Instead, most of the wealth and power the rich were able to hold came from owning real estate. Almost every palatial house had a property a little outside the city where farmers and slaves could cultivate grapes or olives or raise sheep. These properties have not all been discovered, as it is hard to know where they might be located. However, one of these preserved estates has been found a few miles away from the city, and it most likely belonged to the family of Nero's wife, Poppaea Sabina the Younger.

As you can tell, the Romans were very into their food, as even the rich made sure they had their own private stock of it. It can be said that the Romans were also fascinated with their dining habits, as they wrote many of their recipes down, one of which even included bears. It is not known whether the Pompeiians themselves also favored these extravagant menus, but excavations have recovered traces of fish bones, peppercorn, and mint leaves that perfectly fit into a recipe from a Roman cookbook published in the 4th century CE, which was translated from Latin in the Middle Ages.

The recipe stars a rather extravagant dish with the use of herbs and spices: "Ostrich meat, fish sauce, celery seed, roasted cumin, pepper, mint, dates, honey, vinegar, raising vine, and a little olive oil. Place all the ingredients in a pan and bring to a boil. Pour over ostrich meat and serve with sprinkled pepper."

Kitchens, even in the richest homes of Pompeii, could hardly have been equipped and roomy enough to prepare an entire banquet to accommodate guests. For the most part, kitchens mostly occupied small, cramped rooms. There was not much light and featured only basic kitchen equipment, like cauldrons and industrial-size sieves. It is known the rich held lavish banquets, so preparations would have most likely extended to the rest of the house. For example, a slave would prepare food and clean vegetables and fruit on the front steps or in the garden, while the meat would be prepared in front of the guests on portable braziers that would be brought forward for that occasion. Some kitchens were large; for instance, at the Villa of the Mysteries, a kitchen was found that covered a nine-by-twelve-meter area.

The kitchen would have been located on the first floor of a house or villa. Villas had upper floors, but many of these floors were destroyed after the eruption. However, some remained intact, such as Fullonica di Stephanus, which is three stories tall. There, the Romans would have washed their clothes, which was done with a mixture of clay and urine. And while the people waited for their clothes to be washed, they could partake in a snack. Today, you can visit the site to see a recreated kitchen. Historians believe it looks almost exactly as it did almost two thousand years ago.

Going to the dark side of life in Pompeii, it is known that violence and xenophobia took place in the city. While the Roman Empire was brought up with a fusion of multiple cultures, including Egyptian and Greek, not all citizens of Pompeii tolerated foreigners in the city, and some could even be classified as xenophobes. A painting in Pompeii stands as a testimony to the xenophobia present within the walls of the city, despite foreign traders and interactions with foreigners. This painting depicts a made-up scenario involving pygmies (a group of people native to Central Africa) on the Nile. The imagery includes non-flattering scenes, which include group sex and cannibalism, which means someone or several people in Pompeii saw this demographic as savage and primitive, although, in reality, that was not the case at all.

Violent behavior could also be noted through the presence of hooligans invested in the gladiator games and those who engaged in binge drinking in public. One example would be the aforementioned 59 CE incident in the Amphitheatre of Pompeii between the Pompeiians and Nucerians, which Tacitus, a Roman historian, described as a clash of "illegal gangs."

If one ventured to the dark alleys and located an establishment on the corner that looked rather drab, they would have arrived at the ancient brothel of Pompeii. The brothel was decorated with a series of erotic paintings, and it hosted a single lavatory along with five cubicles, where paying customers were satisfied. Hundreds of graffiti samples have been found on the walls of the brothel as a testament to satisfied customers who were more than likely to return. However, the brothel on the corner was not the only place where Pompeiians could pay for sex, for sex workers earned their bread in all kinds of places around the city, which included cramped lodgings and even cafés that sold wine and food. The rich and wealthy, instead of wandering on the city streets, used their slaves for sex services in the comfort of their homes.

It is not known how many slaves lived in Pompeii, but archaeologists and historians suggest that rich and wealthy households had between five to seven slaves, while more impressive households had many more. Slaves would perform various tasks for their masters, from fetching water from the public fountains to cooking, cleaning, shopping, and running other errands. They also fulfilled sexual desires and carried the rich above the mobs in the streets in litters. Slaves lived in cramped lodgings and service rooms in rich households. They would never enter through the main door since that was reserved for the family and their guests; rather, they would go through the side door.

Businesses also employed slaves. For example, fulleries (a shop where clothes were cleaned) depended on slave labor. As mentioned above, Pompeiians used urine as a cleaning agent due to its high concentration of ammonia. Urine would be collected in jars, then taken to the shops. The slaves would spend their time cleaning clothes by standing in small tubs that were filled with a mixture of urine and water, stomping on the clothes to clean them.

Speaking of clothing, slaves could not be immediately recognized by their clothing alone, as they were not distinctive in any way. Actually, slaves wore tunics like their masters, even though Roman citizens could wear togas (they were the only group that could wear them). However, togas could easily get dirty and were hard to clean, so even Roman citizens would stick with tunics.

Slaves were kind of invisible in regards to Roman society. Since slaves were seen as property, they play more of a role in documents and laws than in paintings and mosaics. One of Pompeii's laws states that if a slave was injured by someone's animal, a person, or a passing donkey cart, the slave would be considered "damaged" property, and the party responsible for that damage would need to provide retribution to the owner of said property. It might be hard for us to imagine someone owning another human being and treating them this way, but the practice of slavery was common throughout the world, not just in Rome.

Through the eyes of a slave, Pompeii was not a lavish, breathtaking place with colorful streets and an easygoing life. Some slaves either escaped or tried to escape. Many of those who attempted to break free of their chains were found, with some even being kept in literal chains as punishment. Since the slaves were unable to escape the eruption of Mount Vesuvius, a great number of them were found in prisons designated for slaves during the excavations hundreds of years later.

Slaves did have the potential to become freedmen, which was a status between a slave and a citizen of Rome, although it was possible to become a fully-fledged Roman citizen through formal manumission. A slave could become a freedman by purchasing themselves from their owners or by being freed by the will of their owner.

While slaves performed all kinds of odd jobs and daily tasks for their masters, numerous citizens sought out various professions in Pompeii. Professions like carpenters, painters, innkeepers, architects, perfume sellers, traders, laundrymen, and even pig keepers were, for the most part, considered to be low-income jobs, and former slaves and the poor of Pompeii would tend to be employed in those industries. But what would happen to a Pompeiian who did not have a job? In most cases, these people would work as unskilled laborers, jumping from job to job without any steady income. Romans considered these people to be on the same level as a slave, and for the most part, the comparison was apt, as these jobless people did not have any rights. If one could not work at all, they had to beg in the streets to earn money. Some Pompeiians likely were professional beggars, as some people made decent money from begging in the city of Rome.

One profession that seems to have been favored was that of an artist. Painters and sculptors were busy painting marvelous murals and masterpieces, many of which have been excavated and preserved. The Pompeiians, as well as the Romans in general, loved their art, and artists were painting until the very last day Pompeii breathed life, even seconds before the eruption. In one of the more recently excavated Pompeiian houses, archaeologists discovered an artist frozen in time as he fled from the coming eruption, leaving behind his latest work, the last painting of his four works. Fifty pints of paint, as well as ladders, paintbrushes, and tools of the trade, were discovered at the scene, along with the artist and his assistant, who tried to flee for their lives in the middle of the eruption.

Another prominent profession was in banking, which might be better described as lending. Romans did not have banks or checks, so money lenders were the closest profession to bankers. Lenders would profit on both sides by charging a commission from sellers and by taking a hefty provision from the buyers who borrowed the money.

Male Roman citizens were allowed to vote every year for four officials who would take care of their city's business. There would be two senior officials, who would be in charge of delivering justice, and two junior officials, who would oversee the markets, city property, and streets of Pompeii.

Women did not have that privilege and were not allowed to vote. In general, the women of Pompeii had a major role in domestic life and would take care of their families and households. However, what is known about Pompeiian women is that they had more rights than other women in the ancient world. They were allowed to own property, could have prominent religious roles, and could own a business. Still, most women worked in shops, on farms, as sex workers, or were slaves. Sex workers were mostly female, although there were male prostitutes as well, and they were required to register as prostitutes and pay taxes to the city based on their earnings. However, women's voices could be heard in Pompeii, at least through the wall graffiti. Around 15 percent of election graffiti that was used as political campaigns was written by women.

It was once believed that education was reserved only for those who could afford it and "deserved it," which was essentially the boys from wealthy families. However, partly due to the graffiti found in Pompeii, scholars have realized that most boys of Rome learned the basics of reading and writing, and they could either have gone to school or learned from their parents. Girls also learned how to read and write, but, for the most part, this was reserved for those in the upper classes.

Although working-class Roman boys would go to "school," there was no building built for the specific purpose of educating children. It was possible the boys might have had their parents instruct them, but it was probably more common that they attended an open classroom with other children since their parents were busy from dawn to dusk. These open classrooms had one teacher for reading, writing, and basic arithmetic, and it must have been somewhat distracting to learn in the one in Pompeii as it was located near the Forum, the busiest part of the city. Misbehaving students were disciplined with sticks and would be made an example to the other students to ensure they behaved and paid close attention to their lessons.

Wealthy children were commonly educated by private tutors, with rich families mostly hiring Greek tutors since the Romans respected their culture and saw it as a status symbol to have their children speak and write impeccable Greek.

You can probably already tell, but Romans did not have the same idea of childhood as most modern societies do today. For many today, childhood is a carefree period of our lives, full of fun and painted in innocence. In Pompeii, children were treated almost like adults as soon as they were able to work, and young girls could be married as early as the age of twelve.

When a baby was born to a Pompeiian family, the infant would be wrapped tightly in cloth strips to keep the baby safe. The baby would be placed at the feet of their father, who would be seated when seeing his child for the first time. If the father took the baby and put it on his knees, he was confirming that the baby was his own flesh and blood. If the father did not accept the baby as his, it is possible the disowned infant would be left to die outside the city walls—a cruel practice unimaginable and punishable in modern times.

Since the infant mortality rate was so high, parents would not name their baby for at least a week or two. Many babies would not survive the first two weeks of their short life, while many children would not even survive past childhood. Many diseases that we treat with ease were not treatable in ancient times, hence the high mortality rate among infants and children.

Some girls from lower social classes were taught how to read, write, and do administration work, but for the average Pompeiian family, their daughters would be married off at a young while their sons would become a part of the working class. Girls helped around the house and did chores as soon as they were around seven years old. Some were involved in chores at an even earlier age, pretty much as soon as they could receive instructions and learn from their parents. A girl was expected to take care of her family's home until she was able to have children and marry. While girls could marry at twelve years old, they usually married around the ages of fourteen and fifteen. Having a baby at that age is incredibly stressful on the body, so most girls would die after giving birth to their first child.

Rich families would not always give their daughter's hand as early as a plebian family would, so well-educated, upper-class girls who were unwed mostly spent their time weaving. Upper-class boys would be sent to learn rhetoric at a university, which, again, is not exactly the same as a modern-day university. The boys, who would typically be around the age of fifteen, would be sent abroad, often to Athens or Rhodes. There, they would learn how to become orators and climb the ladder of political success and influence.

You might be wondering if Roman children had any fun growing up. Few toys have been uncovered, but children certainly did not work all hours of the day, every day of the week. For entertainment, they would enjoy the same things their parents did: attend gladiator fights, watch chariot races, and play with dice, to name a few activities. In a way, this exposure at a young age to violent activities as an option for entertainment allowed the bloody practice of fights and races to continue.

Although the lack of a carefree childhood might sound cruel and even disturbing in modern times, family was indeed very important in Pompeii and to ancient Romans. Families lived together and cared for each other, in sickness and in health, while sharing chores, work, and other commitments.

Chapter 6 – The Famous People of Ancient Pompeii

It is not difficult to imagine that some citizens of Pompeii were more popular than others, more appreciated by the general public, or were just lucky enough not to be lost to history after the horrific eruption of Mount Vesuvius covered the city in ash and volcanic debris. With new excavations, some names and buried stories of prominent and famous Pompeiians have been uncovered, allowing us to take a glimpse into their lives and unveil at least some of the Pompeiian mysteries surrounding preserved villas, homes, and documents. These are the people of Pompeii, who may have come from different social classes, professions, and backgrounds but all suffered the same fate long ago.

Lucius Caecilius Iucundus

One of the most notable citizens of Pompeii was Lucius Caecilius Iucundus, who was born to a freedman named Felix. His popularity was not based on his character, of which we know very little, or even his influence, but rather on his notable profession. Lucius was an *argentarius*. Translated from Latin, *argentarius* means "money changer" or "money exchanger," which would be the equivalent to a modern-day moneylender or banker. Romans did not have banks, so citizens relied on professionals like Caecilius, who acted as a middleman in auctions.

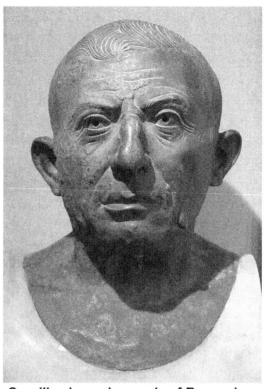

Plaster cast of Lucius Caecilius Iucundus made of Roman bronze and marble, found in the House of Caecilius Iucundus, Pompeii, National Archaeological Museum of Naples.

If someone needed to purchase something from a merchant or pay someone for a service, Caecilius would cover the payment then provide a timeframe for the borrower to return the loan. Caecilius would receive interest on the loans he provided, along with a commission for his services.

What is known about Caecilius's work has been taken from the meticulous records that he kept for all his loans. In these documents, he listed witnesses, names, loan amounts, and other details. By examining these records, historians can see that

Caecilius provided his services to the rich people of Pompeii, as well as other social classes. Caecilius did not work exclusively with Pompeiians or with the rich and wealthy, for the documents found in his house show that he traveled to Nuceria as well, where he helped Publius Alfenus Varus resell a number of slaves that he had previously purchased. The Pompeiian elite seemed to have enjoyed doing business with Caecilius, as many names of rich, noble, and wealthy individuals appear in the documents he left behind. The ancient Romans did not use paper, which was a boon to historians, as paper fades and disintegrates if not kept in the proper conditions. Instead, Caecilius used wax tablets, although wealthy Romans also had access to parchment and papyrus.

Caecilius was a rather interesting figure since he got rich on his wits and became a part of the elite through his name, deeds, and profession, even though his father was once a slave. It is thought that Caecilius did not die in the eruption that swallowed the entire city of Pompeii, as his records stop a few days before the 62 CE earthquake, suggesting that he perished on that day. Caecilius would have been around forty-eight years old when he died.

Poppaea Sabina the Younger

Poppaea Sabina, better known as Poppaea Sabina the Younger to avoid confusing her with her mother of the same name, was born in 30 CE. She was perhaps one of the most influential and most powerful people born and raised in Pompeii. However, she did not spend her entire life in Pompeii or even witnessed the eruption of Vesuvius (she died before it took place).

Poppaea was born to a wealthy and influential family. Her mother, as mentioned above, was Poppaea Sabina the Elder, the daughter of a consul, and her father was Titus Ollius, who was a quaestor, a public official, during the rule of Emperor Tiberius. The family owned magnificent properties in Pompeii and near Herculaneum. Perhaps the family's most well-known villa was Oplontis, which was talked about in a previous chapter. The villa is now known as the Villa

Poppaea. It is also thought that the family owned the House of Menander, which was one of the wealthiest homes in Pompeii. It was named for the well-preserved image of a playwright named Menander, which was found in the house, although some argue the picture does not show Menander but rather the owner of the house reading Menander's works. The house was (and still is) rather impressive, covering 1,800 square meters (19,000 square feet), and it was built to show off the owner's wealth and political influence. And who would be more influential than a family with a long line of influential politicians and members of the Roman elite? Graffiti found by the entrance and elsewhere in the house also point to Poppaea Sabina's family being the owner.

Private baths in the Villa Poppaea. The centerpiece motif painted on the wall shows Hercules in the gardens of Hesperides.

Poppaea was first married to a noble, Rufrius Crispinus, in 44 CE when she was only fourteen years old. Rufrius Crispinus was the leader of the Praetorian Guard for the first ten years of Emperor Claudius's rule (Emperor Claudius was the father of the future emperor, Nero, Poppaea's future husband). A few years after Claudius married Agrippina the Younger, Nero's mother, and she removed Rufrius Crispinus from his position in 51 CE. In 66 CE, Nero, who came to power in 54 CE, had him executed. Poppaea had a son with Rufrius Crispinus, who was named after his deceased father. Nero also killed him, drowning him while they were on a fishing trip (it should be noted this was done much later in Nero's reign, after his mother died).

During Nero's rule, Poppaea married a good friend of the emperor, Otho, who would later become an emperor in 69 CE, ruling for three months as one of the four emperors who took power the year after Nero's death. It is said that Poppaea the Younger married Otho only to get closer to Nero, as she sought to become the empress of Rome. The ambitious Poppaea eventually succeeded in her mission, as she managed to make Nero fall in love with her and allowed her to become his mistress even though she was still married to his friend Otho. In either 58 or 59 CE, Otho and Poppaea were divorced, and Otho was sent to the Roman province of Lusitania to become its governor, allowing Poppaea to focus on her goal of becoming the empress and Nero's wife.

At the time, Nero was married to his stepsister, Claudia Octavia, the daughter of the late Emperor Claudius, Agrippina's husband. As the Roman historian Tacitus claims, Poppaea's next scheme involved pressuring Nero to kill his mother so she could marry him since Agrippina would have been a direct threat to Poppaea's influence on Nero. Modern historians, however, consider that Nero's motives to kill his mother were, in reality, enticed by Agrippina's plans to set her second cousin, Gaius Rubellius Plautus, on the throne. Plautus was

Nero's greatest political opponent, and by helping him plot his way to the throne, Agrippina signed her death warrant, which would be served by her son in 59 CE.

Now that Agrippina was gone, Poppaea had a clear path to pressure Nero to divorce Claudia Octavia so he could marry her instead. However, Nero did not marry Poppaea until 62 CE. This marriage came about after Poppaea was with child, after which he divorced Claudia and married Poppaea twelve days later. He exiled Claudia and sent her to Campania near Pompeii, then sent her to the island of Pandateria (modern-day Ventotene). Pandateria was a common location for banished members of the royal family who had committed adultery. However, Nero never accused Claudia Octavia of adultery, instead claiming she was barren and unable to grant him children and an heir to the throne.

In 63 CE, Poppaea gave birth to a girl and named her Claudia Augusta. The baby died when she was only four months old. "Augusta" was an honorable title that Nero granted to his daughter and his second wife, Poppaea, as soon as the little girl was born.

Nero's rule was marked by debauchery, extravagance, and the persecution of Christians, and he was greatly influenced by Poppaea, which was why the two probably were not Rome's favorite couple. For instance, it is thought that Poppaea intervened in the case of prohibiting gladiator games for ten years in Pompeii after the incident between the Nucerians and Pompeiians, convincing Nero to allow games before the expiration of the decade-long prohibition. If this is true, then Poppaea had an immense influence on Nero even when she was nothing but his mistress. It seems that Poppaea had a talent for playing political games. She was often described by contemporary historians as a beautiful woman who used schemes and intrigue to become the empress and get whatever she wanted.

Poppaea regularly resided in Rome with her husband, but she would frequently visit the villa today known as the Villa of Poppaea.

In 65 CE, Poppaea was awaiting the birth of her second child with Nero. This was also the year of Poppaea's sudden death. Many writers and historians of the time blamed Nero for Poppaea's death, claiming that he either poisoned his wife or kicked her in the stomach during a quarrel. Cassius Dio, a Roman historian, who was biased and formed a negative opinion about Nero based on his imperial rule, claimed that Nero leaped upon her belly, either unintentionally or on purpose, which caused her to die from pregnancy complications. Modern historians argue that Poppaea might have died during childbirth since she might have had a stillborn or miscarriage in the last weeks of her pregnancy.

If one was to judge whether Nero did it or not based on his mourning alone, one would conclude that he did not have anything to do with Poppaea's death. He went into a deep depression, and he gave her an extravagant state funeral. According to Tacitus, she was even embalmed, even though cremation was the custom at the time, with her body being filled with herbs and spices and buried in the Tomb of the Julii. However, Poppaea's body was not found there, so the place of her burial remains a mystery.

Aulus Vettius Restitutus and Aulus Vettius Conviva

The names of Aulus Vettius Restitutus and Aulus Vettius Conviva were uncovered with the excavations of the House of the Vettii hundreds of years after the deadly eruption. The House of the Vettii, which was mentioned in a previous chapter, is one of the most imposing and wealthiest properties discovered in Pompeii, which makes it somewhat strange that this villa belonged to two freedmen of the Vettii family who had been either lucky or smart enough to become wealthy after they were granted freedom. The House of the Vettii testifies that its owners were extremely wealthy. Although some of the paintings have been lost, twelve mythological scenes were preserved.

Restitutus and Conviva were related, but their relationship has not been clarified. They might have been brothers or cousins. Conviva belonged to the Brotherhood of Augustus, carrying the title of an Augustalis. The Brotherhood of Augustus was an order of priests originally appointed by the second Roman emperor, Tiberius, who ruled the empire from 14 CE to 37 CE. The order was supposed to maintain the cult of Julii, one of the oldest patrician families, and the cult of Augustus, the first emperor of the Roman Empire. Conviva's name even appears in receipts and documents found in the home of Lucius Caecilius Iucundus. Conviva donated a large sum to be used for public work projects, which hints that the Vettii did not build a splendid villa to display their riches but were genuinely wealthy and contributed to the city with their financial power.

The story of the Vettii is not entirely revealed to us, except for the fact that Conviva and Restitutus were related and were once slaves who managed to earn the status of freedmen and become wealthy merchants. Thus, their story (what is known of it, at least) is a perfect example of the mobility of social classes in Pompeii and Rome at the time. The theory is that the Vettii brothers became rich by selling wine, and in time, they were able to earn the status of being part of the wealthy middle class. Since Conviva was an Augustalis, he was most likely closer to the status of nobility than of the wealthy middle class.

Julia Felix

Julia Felix was the owner of a large property in Pompeii, which was named after her when archaeologists unveiled the house during the excavations that began in 1755. Julia Felix lived in a large house located on the Via dell'Abbondanza. It was originally her home until she converted some of the rooms to apartments, which she rented after the earthquake of 62 CE. The location itself and the size of the property speaks in favor of Julia's wealth. But who was Julia Felix? Was she a noblewoman, a wife of a prominent politician, or perhaps a daughter of a Pompeiian merchant?

Unfortunately, we do not know who Julia Felix actually was, but we do know that she was a savvy businesswoman and a prominent public figure. Some scholars suggest that Julia was a low-born daughter, possibly even born out of wedlock, while others think she might have been from the imperial elite and somehow inherited the wealth she later multiplied with her clever business tactics. Others suggest that Julia was a descendant of an imperial freedman, which would once again demonstrate the rise of the new middle class.

As you can see, little is known about Julia's past and early life. Still, the preserved home reveals that Julia became a public figure in Pompeii, who generated more wealth by renting apartments and installing gardens for public use, as well as building luxurious baths she most likely rented to elite Pompeiians. Renting the baths to the elite would have given her a great fortune at the time since most public baths were closed for repairs after the 62 CE earthquake.

In ancient Rome, women were not allowed to own property unless they had a legal male guardian in their life. Some noblewomen, however, could own houses and lands if they were independent of their husbands, fathers, or other legal guardian, which lends credence to the idea that Julia came from a noble family since she was the sole owner of the villa. However, there is strong evidence that suggests she came from a lower class. The inscription on the entrance of her estate reads, "To let, in the estate of Julia Felix, the daughter of Spurius: elegant baths for respectable people, shops with upper rooms, and apartments. From 13th August next to 13th August of the sixth year, for five continuous years. The lease will expire at the end of five years." Sprurius was not actually a person; rather, the phrase "daughter of Spurius" means she was born out of wedlock. In addition to this, Liisa Savunen, a scholar of Roman history, suggests the name Julia indicates that she or her father might have been a slave, as "most of the Julii in Pompeii were imperial freedmen and their descendants."

Eumachia

Eumachia was a priestess of the imperial cult in Pompeii. She was a prominent and rich woman who earned respect and admiration through her devotion to the city of Pompeii and its citizens. She also draws her origins from one of the oldest families in the city.

Wealthy women from prominent families in ancient Rome could not become politicians, but they could still have important roles in religion and religious cults. Eumachia was the matron of Concordia Augustus, which was a cult that honored the deified Roman emperor Augustus. She was also the matron of the Fullers guild (a *fullo* was a Roman laundry worker). There were several fulleries, also known as *fullonica* in Latin, around the city of Pompeii, and the rich would build *fullonica* as a part of their estate, employing slaves as laundry workers.

By WolfgangRieger - Filippo Coarelli (ed.): Pompeji. Hirmer, München 2002, ISBN 3-7774-9530-1, p. 137, Public Domain. The man on the left is brushing a wool cloth, and the man on the right is whitening fabrics beneath a caged dome. On top of the cage is an owl, which represents Athena, who was the goddess protector of wool merchants.

https://commons.wikimedia.org/wiki/File:Pompeii_-_Fullonica_of_Veranius_Hypsaeus_1_-_MAN.jpg

Eumachia was a prominent public figure, which went hand in hand with her status and her good deeds as a benefactor. In fact, Eumachia used part of her wealth to build the east side of the Forum in Pompeii, which may have been a building for the Fullers guild since the building contained a statue of her.

This building is also significant since it allows us to find out more about Eumachia's life through a dedicatory inscription. She was a daughter of Lucius and a priestess, and she also had a son named Marcus Numistrius Fronto. The name of her son might have been mentioned to set up a fruitful terrain for him in case he ever decided to enter politics.

Eumachia is a perfect example of how a woman could get involved in social politics and the public life of Pompeii.

Chapter 7 – The Last Days in Pompeii before the Eruption

Seventeen years before the people of Pompeii would live their last days on Earth, a devastating earthquake turned half the city into rubble. If the people of ancient Pompeii knew that the earthquake was, in reality, announcing the eruption of Mount Vesuvius, they would have probably left before it was too late to save themselves. It would have been difficult for the rich and wealthy to leave everything they had behind, such as their luxurious villas, magnificent artwork, paintings, precious possessions, and even the beautiful city of Pompeii, the jewel in the crown of the Roman Empire, but at least they would leave with their lives. Unfortunately, nobody knew what the earthquake was foretelling.

The earthquake in 62 CE was strong and horrific, and it destroyed buildings in Pompeii as well as the neighboring city of Herculaneum. The aftershocks shook the ground for days after the main quake. Seneca the Younger, a Roman philosopher, statesman, and dramatist, wrote that a flock of six hundred sheep died due to the poisonous fumes that appeared due to the earthquake.

Seneca the Younger wrote about the effects of earthquakes in the sixth book of his *Naturales quaestiones*, attributing the devastating force of the earthquake, which happened on February 5th, 62 CE, to the movement of the air. It is hard to know for certain if Mount Vesuvius caused the earthquake or not, but it certainly was catastrophic. Most scholars believe that it registered at between 5 and 6.1 in magnitude, although some estimates go as high as 7.5. In his work, Seneca touched upon how terrifying an earthquake can be:

"What hiding-place will creatures find, where will they flee in their anxiety, if fear arises from below and is drawn from the depths of the earth? There is panic on the part of all when buildings creak and give signs of falling. Then everybody hurls himself headlong outside, abandons his household possessions, and trusts to his luck in the outdoors. What hiding-place do we look to, what help, if the earth itself is causing the ruin, if what protects us, upholds us, on which cities are built, which some speak of as a kind of foundation of the universe, separates and reels?"

After the ground had settled and the damage had been assessed, the citizens of Pompeii started to rebuild. Many of the wealthy citizens decided to leave, allowing the rich middle class to take their place at the top of the totem pole. Repairing the city was a slow and lengthy process. As might be expected, the most affected were the poor, whose homes were almost entirely destroyed. Businesses like the one conducted by Julia Felix would have boomed since people would have been looking for accommodations and a place to live until their homes could be rebuilt. It is less likely that the poor could afford to stay at the Felix villa, but the rich who remained in the city would have found comfort in the luxurious baths of the prominent house. Nero gave money to Rome to help with the repairs since his wife, Poppaea Sabina the Younger, had once called the city home.

Only two years later, in 64 CE, another earthquake shook the region, affecting Pompeii once again. However, it was nowhere near as devastating as the first one. The earthquake was recorded by Suetonius, a Roman historian, as well as by Tacitus, who also wrote about Emperor Nero's first performance in the grand theater of Naples. Suetonius wrote about Nero's performance as well, which took place during the earthquake itself, noting that Nero continued to sing on stage even though the ground had started to shake. The emperor would not leave the stage until he had finished the song, and as Tacitus and Suetonius both remarked, the theater collapsed moments after the emperor and the auditorium had been evacuated.

By the time of the eruption in 79 CE, the city was mostly rebuilt, although there was still plenty of buildings that remained damaged. It is not likely that the Pompeiians were aware of the far greater threat that was about to swallow the entire city and freeze it in time.

Instead, life in the city went on with its usual routines, even though there was a series of earthquakes four days before the eruption in 79 CE.

As Pliny the Younger, a prominent magistrate and author, noted, the people of Campania were so accustomed to earthquakes that they considered it to be a normal thing, not even suspecting that Vesuvius was about to erupt. Pliny the Younger was in Pompeii before the eruption, although he was just a teenager, and his letters to Tacitus, which he wrote about twenty-five years after the event, would be perhaps the most fateful testimony to what the final days of Pompeii looked like.

Thus, the Pompeiians decided to dismiss the violent warnings that continued for four days before the eruption, perhaps even setting up a celebration for Vulcanalia. Vulcanalia was a festival that was

celebrated every year on August 23rd. Ironically enough, it was dedicated to the god of fire and volcanos, Vulcan, meaning he would have been the god to protect the people of Pompeii from the destruction that was about to ensue. Vulcan, who is known as Hephaestus in Greek mythology, was also a skillful master of metalworking. To celebrate Vulcan, Pompeiians would set up large bonfires around the city and displayed shrines dedicated to the god. They held numerous games to celebrate the god of fire and volcanoes while offering sacrifices to please him. They also threw live fish and small animals into the fire during the festivities.

It is possible this festival took place either a day or two days before the eruption, and if that was the case, the volcano would have been showing some signs of life. There would have been small earthquakes and smoke, but because of the festival, the people would have seen these as good signs that Vulcan was busy working on his forge on Mount Vesuvius.

Statuette of Vulcan, the god of fire, volcanoes, and metalworking, created

approximately around the 1st century CE, bronze. Photo credits: By Marie-Lan Nguyen, 2008-12-26, CC BY 2.5.

However, it is hard to know exactly when the eruption happened. Pliny the Younger wrote letters to Tacitus around twenty-five years after the eruption, and in them, he states the eruption took place on August 24th. As time has passed, scholars believe the date was copied incorrectly and that it could have been a variety of different dates, such as October 30th or November 23rd. This variety in dates is due to the Romans' convention for calendar dates, which can be somewhat difficult to follow.

Beginning in the 18th century, scholars began to suggest that the eruption happened after August 24th, although this theory was not fully embraced until recently. In 2007, scientists concluded that the debris pattern of the eruption is more consistent with the winds in the fall than in the late summer. In 2018, archaeologists found an inscription that was dated October 17th. Since the inscription is thought to not have been older than 79 CE, that means October 18th, 79 CE, is the earliest possible date for the eruption of Mount Vesuvius, although historians think it took place later in the month or even in November.

Chapter 8 – The Eruption of Mount Vesuvius and the Demise of Pompeii

On the day of the eruption, the people of Pompeii rose with the sun to catch the first glimpses of daylight just as they would do any other day. They would have had breakfast, went to the market, visited shops, and went to work. Aside from the minor tremors they would have felt and were already accustomed to, it seemed like an ordinary day.

Pliny the Younger, who was born around 61 CE, was seventeen years old when the eruption took place. His uncle on his mother's side, who was called Pliny the Elder, was the commander of a Roman fleet stationed at Misenum, which was a part of the Italian province of Naples and one of the naval bases of the Roman Empire.

The letters that Pliny the Younger wrote to Tacitus describing the last day of Pompeii as Pliny knew it represent a rich source of information on how the most horrific volcanic eruption in Europe destroyed a strategically and economically important city of Campania.

The Last Day of Pompeii, oil on canvas, Karl Bryullov, created 1830–1833. Bryullov visited Pompeii in 1828 and made sketches depicting the eruption in 79 CE that destroyed Pompeii. He later painted this work, which is considered to be one of his greatest works of art. It later inspired Edward Bulwer-Lytton's book, The Last Days of Pompeii.

Pliny the Younger notes in his letters to Tacitus that his mother had noticed a massive, unusual cloud appearing around Mount Vesuvius. As Pliny the Younger records, the cloud must have appeared around the seventh hour of the day, which would have been around noon. Ash carried by the winds soon appeared near Pompeii. It was not clear to Pliny's mother or Pliny's uncle, who, in addition to being a naval commander, was a naturalist (perhaps one of the greatest of ancient Rome), that the first phase of the eruption had already commenced. At this point, Vesuvius was ejecting hot gases high into the stratosphere while also ejecting volcanic debris. Pliny the Younger describes the first hours of the eruption like so: "On the 24th of August, about one in the afternoon, my mother desired him [Pliny the Elder] to observe a cloud which appeared of very unusual size and shape. He had just taken a turn in the sun, and, after bathing himself in cold water, and making a light luncheon, gone back to his books: he immediately arose and went out upon a rising ground from whence he might get a better sight of this very uncommon appearance. A cloud, from which mountain was uncertain, at this distance (but it was found afterward to come from Mount Vesuvius), was ascending, the appearance of which I cannot give you a more exact description of than by likening it to that of a pine-tree, for it shot up to a great height in the form of a very tall trunk, which spread itself out at the top into a sort of branches; occasioned, I imagine, either by a sudden gust of air that impelled it, the force of which decreased as it advanced upwards, or the cloud itself, being pressed back again by its weight, expanded in the manner I have mentioned; it appeared sometimes bright and sometimes dark and spotted, according to as it was either more or less impregnated with earth and cinders. This phenomenon seemed to a man of such learning and research as my uncle extraordinary and worth further looking into."

What may not be clear at first when reading one of the 247 surviving letters (it is thought many more were sent) that Pliny the Younger wrote to his friend and historian Tacitus is the phrase "He had just taken a turn in the sun." The phrase refers to the ancient Roman practice of walking and sunbathing naked in the sun while covering one's body in oils. This was considered to be healthy, and Roman men would practice this routine daily. The fact that Pliny the Elder would take a turn in the sun, bathe, and then have lunch tells us that he was not aware of the danger the city was facing at that moment.

Around one p.m., ash and pumice started to fall upon Pompeii. It is believed that the accumulations were between ten and fifteen centimeters (between four and six inches) per hour. By five p.m., there was a layer of pumice 280 centimeters (a little over nine feet) thick. A roof even collapsed under the weight of ash and pumice stone, and it was just the first of many. By this point, there was no natural light left. Dogs were howling and barking, people were screaming and fleeing, while some were killed by collapsing buildings and the volcanic stones falling upon the city.

Before the pumice and ash would start to cover the city entirely, Pliny the Elder was already heading with the galleys under his command to help the cities and people who were close to Vesuvius. The wife of Bassus, Rectina, who was mentioned in the letters, feared the imminent danger since she was stranded in Stabiae, which was about sixteen kilometers (nine miles) from Mount Vesuvius. As Pliny the Elder rushed to aid Rectina and others who were in danger, pieces of cinder and hot black stones fell on the ships' decks. Instead of docking at Herculaneum, which had seen little ash fall, Pliny the Elder steered to Stabiae. He could not dock to meet Rectina, though, and it is unknown if she made it out alive.

However, Pliny did make it to Stabiae, where he met his friend Pomponianus, a Roman senator who witnessed the eruption, assuring him that everything would be all right and that fortune favored the brave. According to Pliny the Younger's letters, Pliny the Elder was stuck at his friend's villa due to the winds. So, he decided to make the best of it. He bathed and had supper with Pomponianus. The sunlight was slowly leaving the sky as evening fell, and the night emphasized the brightness and clearness of the flames, which came out of several sides of Vesuvius.

Pliny the Younger could see the flames from Misenum, as well as the groups of people escaping and fleeing, some without any belongings. However, many Pompeiians remained in the city. It is known based on the excavations that took place centuries later that there were at least two thousand people in Pompeii who sought shelter in the cellars of various buildings, hoping they would be able to wait out the danger.

The eruption continued throughout the night. At around eleven p.m., the first surge hit Herculaneum and neighboring cities. At this point, the Pompeiians still had a chance to flee from the imminent danger, but many of those remaining in the city chose to stay.

John Martin, 1821, The Destruction of Pompeii and Herculaneum, the restored version.

https://commons.wikimedia.org/wiki/File:Destruction_of_Pompeii_and_Herculaneum.jpg

Fear among the people grew with the view of the night sky, which was almost swallowed by the fire coming from Vesuvius. Around midnight, the column above Vesuvius reached thirty-three kilometers (twenty miles) in the air. In the next seven hours, six pyroclastic surges would strike the vicinity. Pyroclastic surges are clouds of ash, rock, and volcanic gas that stick low to the ground and move with hurricane-like winds. The temperatures of these surges would hit several hundred degrees on both the Celsius and Fahrenheit scales. It is more likely that the heat killed the people rather than burning in lava, which never actually made its way to Pompeii, or from being covered by ash while still alive. A leading volcanologist named Giuseppe Mastrolorenzo states that "temperatures outdoors—and indoors—rose up to 300°C [570°F] and more, enough to kill hundreds of people in a fraction of a second...when the pyroclastic surge hit Pompeii, there was no time to suffocate...The contorted postures are not the effects of a long agony, but of the cadaveric spasm, a consequence of heat shock on corpses."

Around one a.m., Herculaneum was destroyed with the first pyroclastic surge. It is estimated that the surge measured between 400 and 450 degrees Celsius (752 and 842 degrees Fahrenheit). It was so hot that wood and leather were carbonized, and the flesh of those still alive burned right off.

Pompeii was the next major city to be hit. Around 6:30 a.m., a pyroclastic surge hit the city. This surge was not as hot as the one at Herculaneum. Instead of burning the bodies, a hard shell was formed around them, which allowed archaeologists to make the famous body casts of those who died in the eruption.

Pliny the Elder and his friend, Pomponianus, were still alive at this time. Sometime during the night or early morning (possibly even shortly after the people of Pompeii were wiped out), the house shook awake those inside (if they had even fallen asleep to begin with), and they had to make the fateful decision as to whether they should stay or make a run for it. They decided to leave, strapping pillows on their head to try and somewhat protect themselves from the falling stones.

Pliny the Younger and his mother also fled from Misenum, and they were lucky enough to find safety. Pliny the Elder was not so lucky. The following is how Pliny the Younger believed events played out in regards to his uncle's death.

"It was now day everywhere else, but there deeper darkness prevailed than in the thickest night; which, however, was in some degree alleviated by torches and other lights of various kinds. They thought it proper to go farther down upon the shore to see if they might safely put out to sea, but found the waves still running extremely high, and boisterous. There my uncle, laying himself down upon sailcloth, which was spread for him, called twice for some cold water, which he drank, when immediately the flames, preceded by a strong whiff of sulfur, dispersed the rest of the party, and obliged him to rise. He raised himself up with the assistance of two of his servants and instantly fell dead; suffocated, as I conjecture, by some gross and noxious vapor, having always had a weak throat, which was often inflamed. As soon as it was light again, which was not till the third day after this melancholy accident, his body was found entire, and without any marks of violence upon it, in the dress in which he fell, and looking more like a man asleep than dead."

The Aftermath

Just as we are simultaneously fascinated and horrified by this horrendous event, the Romans were perhaps in an even greater state of shock. Judging by the large number of written documents that recorded the events in Pompeii and the effects that the eruption left on Campania and, with it, on the Roman Empire, this event left a strong and deeply emotional and physical imprint on Rome. The process of healing would be long and hard considering that entire cities were destroyed, along with agriculture and the economy of Campania. It would take a lot of time for the region to recover, and the wound left in the empire's collective memory was deep, and it slowly healed. As a testimony of that impact, many Roman authors and historians wrote about the event, among which are Pliny the Younger's letters.

The Roman statesman and historian Cassius Dio also wrote about the eruption, which is mostly veiled in superstition:

"Many huge men, greater than human size, as giants are depicted, made an appearance, now on the mountain, now in the surrounding countryside and the cities, wandering day and night on the earth and passing through the air. After this were terrible droughts and sudden violent earthquakes, so that the whole plain seethed and the summits leaped up, there were roars, some underground like thunder, some on the surface like the bellowing of oxen. The sea too roared and the sky re-echoed it. Then a sudden portentous crash was heard as if the mountains were collapsing, and first enormous stones were thrown up to reach the height of the mountain-tops themselves, then great quantity of fire and endless smoke so that the whole sky was shaded, the sun completely hidden as if eclipsed.

So day became night, light darkness. Some thought the giants were rising in revolt (for many of their forms could be seen through the smoke, and in addition a sound of trumpets was heard). Others thought that the whole universe was being consumed by chaos or fire. Therefore they fled, some from their houses into the streets, some from outside indoors; from the sea inland and from there to the sea, since in their confusion, they thought that wherever they were not was safer than where they were. At the same time, an unbelievable quantity of ash was blown out, covering land, sea, and all the sky. Not surprisingly, it did a great deal of damage to men, farms, and cattle. It destroyed all fish and birds and, in addition, it buried two whole cities, Herculaneum and Pompeii, while its population was sitting in the theatre. The whole cloud of dust was so great that some of it reached Africa, Syria, and Egypt; it also reached Rome, filling the sky above it and darkening the sun. It occasioned no little fear for several days since people did not know and could not imagine what had happened, but thought that everything was being turned upside down and that the sun was vanishing into the earth and the earth being lifted into the heavens. However, this ash did them no great damage, but later brought a terrible plague on them."

At the time of the eruption, Titus had been the emperor of the Roman Empire for a few months, and he was judged by the way he helped those affected by this horrific natural disaster. It was not an uncommon thing for Rome to aid its colonies and cities that suffered a disaster, and Titus's reign was tested by many disasters as Suetonius and Cassius Dio both describe:

"In his reign, several dreadful disasters occurred—an eruption of Mount Vesuvius in Campania, a fire at Rome that burned for three days and nights, and one of the worst ever outbreaks of the plague. In the face of all these disasters, he displayed not merely the concern of an emperor but also the deep love of a father, whether by offering messages of sympathy or by giving all the financial help he could. He selected by lot some senators of consular rank to regenerate Campania, and allocated the property of those who had died in the eruption and who had no surviving heirs to the renewal of the afflicted towns."

- **Suetonius**

"In the following year, a fire on the ground spread over a very large part of Rome while Titus was away following the disaster in Campania…Titus, therefore, sent two ex-consuls to Campania to refound the settlements and gave money and the possessions of those who had died without heirs. Titus himself took no money from individuals or cities or kings although many kept giving and promising him large sums, but restored all the damage from his resources."

- **Cassius Dio**

The excavations of Pompeii have uncovered 1,150 bodies, although it is estimated that 2,000 people died in the eruption. The excavations have demonstrated the power of nature and have also unveiled the once wealthy and beautiful city of Pompeii. Pompeii still holds unearthed secrets, so excavations continue to this day, revealing more mysteries of antiquity. Today, Pompeii stands as a powerful source of knowledge about the lives of the Roman people and those of other cultures who were subdued by the Roman Republic and, later, the Roman Empire.

Conclusion

In the centuries following the eruption, the name and location of Pompeii were lost. The first known year of someone stumbling onto Pompeii was 1592. Domenico Fontana, an architect, discovered paintings while digging an aqueduct. However, he kept the news to himself, so no one investigated the area to see what else could be uncovered. In 1738, men found Herculaneum while settling the foundations for a royal palace. This discovery led archaeologists to find other cities that had been affected by the eruption, even though they did not know the names of the places for which they were searching. In 1763, an inscription was found that identified the city as Pompeii.

Although the city had been forgotten, once it was rediscovered, people were fascinated by the site and the tragic fate that befell its people. And as the discoveries continued, people found more reasons to fall in love with the city. Its origins date as far back as the

8th century BCE, and it was home to wealthy individuals who essentially treated the city as their summer vacation spot.

Pompeii is now one of the most visited archaeological sites in the world, and it is listed as a UNESCO World Heritage Site. Pompeii is still revealing its secrets through its art, artifacts, architecture, and people, some of whose lives and names survived the tooth of time. The last series of excavations took place in 2018, and the archaeologists targeted locations around the city, and it resulted in new findings of historical importance.

Our fascination with Pompeii and the sympathy we have with those who lost their lives coincides with the terror we feel when trying to imagine how the fateful day of the eruption must have played out. Pompeii remains one of the most important archaeological sites, as it provides detailed examples of Roman life, culture, architecture, and history. The communities of the city were comprised of a multitude of different cultures, and it is certain that the excavations will continue to reward us with discoveries and a more complete understanding of antiquity and the people who lived during that time.